Decorative Painting

FOR HOME & GARDEN

Decorative Painting

FOR HOME & GARDEN

Karen Embry

Sterling Publishing Co., Inc.
New York

Prolific Impressions Production Staff:

Editor in Chief: Mickey Baskett
Copy Editor: Phyllis Mueller
Graphics: Dianne Miller, Karen Turpin
Photography: Rob Bovarnick with Rob/Harris Productions, Tampa, FL
   (813) 258-4061.
Administration: Jim Baskett

Every effort has been made to insure that the information presented is accurate. Since we have no control over physical conditions, individual skills, or chosen tools and products, the publisher disclaims any liability for injuries, losses, untoward results, or any other damages which may result from the use of the information in this book. Thoroughly read the instructions for all products used to complete the projects in this book, paying particular attention to all cautions and warnings shown for that product to ensure their proper and safe use.

Library of Congress Cataloging-in-Publication Data:
Embry, Karen.
  Decorative painting for home & garden / Karen Embry.
     p. cm.
  Includes index.
  ISBN 1-4027-0643-X
  1. Painting. 2. Decoration and ornament. 3. Garden ornaments and furniture.
  I. Title.
  TT385.E46 2003
  745.7'23--dc22

2003014298

10 9 8 7 6 5 4 3 2 1

Published by Sterling Publishing Co., Inc.
387 Park Avenue South, New York, N.Y. 10016

© 2003 by Prolific Impressions, Inc.

Produced by Prolific Impressions, Inc.
160 South Candler St., Decatur, GA 30030

Distributed in Canada by Sterling Publishing
c/o Canadian Manda Group, One Atlantic Avenue, Suite 105
Toronto, Ontario, Canada M6K 3E7
Distributed in Great Britain by Chrysalis Books
64 Brewery Road, London N7 9NT, England
Distributed in Australia by Capricorn Link (Australia) Pty. Ltd.
P.O. Box 704, Windsor, NSW 2756 Australia

ACKNOWLEDGEMENTS

Thanks to:
For FolkArt® Acrylic Paints, Mod Podge® decoupage medium, and FolkArt Sealers
Plaid Enterprises
3225 Westech Drive
Norcross, Georgia 30092
800-842-4197
www.plaidonline.com

For the bedside table, four drawer cabinet, toy chest, drop leaf table, and wall shelf
Walnut Hollow
1409 State Road 23
Dodgeville, WI 53533-2112
800-944-2331
www.walnuthollow.com
e-mail: creative@walnuthollow.com

For the garden bench
Viking Woodcrafts
1317 8th Street SE
Waseca, MN 56093
800-328-0116
www.vikingwoodcrafts.com

For paint brushes
Silver Brush Limited
P. O. Box 414
Windsor, NJ 08561-4888
609-443-4900
www.silverbrush.com
e-mail: customerservice@silverbrush.com

For bead fringe
Expo International
Houston, TX 77036-2105
www.expointl.com

For swing and fireplace screen
Wood Creations
Tom Mingolello
Palm Harbor, Florida
727-455-5539
e-mail: Woodbytom@aol.com

For the canvas pillow cover
BagWorks Inc.
3301-C South Cravens Road
Fort Worth, TX 76119
800-365-7423
www.bagworks.com
e-mail: info@bagworks.com

For the Adirondack chair
SMI of Ohio
P. O. Box 3400
Columbus, OH 43234-0041

For UV Resistant Matte Spray Finish
Krylon Products Group
101 Prospect Avenue, NW
Cleveland, Ohio 44115
800-797-3332
www.krylon.com

For the arch-top mirror
Bear Creek Woodworks
217-223-0082
Quincy, IL

For trinket boxes
Bear With Us
3007 So. Kendal Avenue
Independence, MO 64055
816-373-3231
bearwus@aol.com

For stains, sealers, wood filler, varnish, primer, and wood sealer
J.W. etc. Fine Quality Products
2205 First Street
Suite 103
Simi Valley, CA 93065
805-526-5066
www.jwetc.com

For Perm Enamel Paints
Delta Technical Coatings, Inc.
2550 Pellissier Place
Whittier, CA 90601
800-423-4135
www.deltacrafts.com

For the twig bench and wooden bar stool
Fergie's Tole Shop
Pat and Sharon Ferguson
8730 49th Street N., Suite 4
Pinellas Park, FL 33782
727-545-3713
www.fergiestoleshop.com
e-mail: PatFergy@aol.com

Dedication

Often we lose sight of what is really important in our everyday lives. When all is said and done, it is all about the people we love, the time we share, and the memories we make. So to my family I dedicate this book, with love.

Karen

About the Author

Karen Howell Embry is an artist, designer, teacher, and author. Her love of drawing and painting began as a child, and her father, a commercial artist, was a great influence on her creative spirit.

Born in Tampa, Florida, she attended the University of South Florida and has been teaching painting for almost 20 years. As well as designing, she also has a decorative painting business, Karen Embry Designs, specializing in murals and faux finishes. Karen has had several decorative painting project books published by Plaid Enterprises and many of her projects have been published in multi-author books and magazines. She is a member of the Society of Craft Designers (SCD), Society of Decorative Painters (SDP), Stencil Artisans League (SALI), Hobby Industry Association (HIA), and Association of Craft and Creative Industries (ACCI).

Karen still resides in Tampa with her husband Chuck, daughter Davi, and son Kyle.

A Word From Karen Embry

I believe I am blessed to work in a profession that I truly enjoy as an artist and designer. The journey that brought me to this point in my life has had its challenges as well as its rewards. I believe in dreams and finding your passion. If you believe with your whole heart and soul, then anything is possible.

From an early age I knew that I wanted to be an artist. I think that I always looked at people and things in my surroundings differently – analyzing them and seeing them not for what they were, but for what they could be. I suppose that being headstrong and persistent are good qualities, but I'm sure that I was a handful for my parents! What I know for sure (thanks, Oprah!) is that the unconditional love and support of my family has been a tremendous asset in accomplishing my goals and dreams. They make it matter.

Special Thanks

- **To my parents, Gene and Ida Howell**: The best parents ever! You always encouraged and supported me as well as all of my creative endeavors. I love you and thank you for everything that you've done!

- To my daughter, **Davi**, and my son, **Kyle**: Words can hardly begin to express how proud I am to be your mom. With all my heart I love you two for the laughter, excitement, and happiness you bring to my life. I am grateful for all of the times you understood when I spent so much time working in the studio. It's great seeing the world through the eyes of teenagers.

- To my husband **Chuck**: You keep it all together and always seem to make everything all right. Your endless patience in tolerating the confusion, clutter, deadlines, and simple craziness of being married to an artist is more than I could ever ask! You have always believed in me and my dreams, and you have my heart forever. Love you.

- **And to the rest of my family** – Kathy, Mario, Jose, and Christina Tamayo, my in-laws Ken and Betty Embry, Tim, Tonya, Victoria, and Whitney Embry: Thank you for your enthusiasm and encouragement.

- **To my friends and students**: Thanks for listening and sharing ideas and good times, but mostly for making me laugh.

- To **Mickey Baskett**, my editor: My sincerest gratitude for your faith in my talent and the opportunity to work with you on this book.

No matter what your decorating style, painted furniture and accessories add personal style to your décor. Whether inside or out, a decorative painted piece says something about your creativity and love of art. Because of the popularity of painted pieces in home decorating today, painted pieces have become very costly to buy – both new and antique. Painting your own pieces is the solution.

With all the wonderful ideas, instructions, and patterns in this book, you have the ability at your fingertips to create your own one of a kind painted pieces to decorate your garden and your home. Artist, Karen Embry has created painted pieces for this book with a fun and whimsical folk art look. The pieces are practical, useful, and will add just the right bit of panache to your décor.

You will be amazed at how easy these designs are to paint. Karen's illustrative style creates the foundation, and her color sense pulls the look together. Her painting style is very easy to emulate. There are just a few "painterly" techniques to master – and those are all explained in word and step-by-step photos. Once you have transferred the pattern to your piece of furniture, just follow the color placement instructions, add a few shadows and highlights as explained – and you will be amazed at what you have painted. And your friends and family will be so impressed.

I enjoyed working on this book because the designs made me so happy. They have such a light-hearted look - you can't help but smile when you look at the beautiful garden angel, or the charming snowmen. And who wouldn't be inspired by the garden bench, or feel like a queen when sitting on the Queen of Hearts chair. Each piece is unique. I hope you enjoy recreating the designs Karen Embry has created for you.

Mickey Baskett, editor

SUPPLIES

Paints, Mediums, & Finishes

◆ ACRYLIC CRAFT PAINTS

Acrylic craft paints, which were used to paint all of the wooden pieces in this book, come in a wide array of pre-mixed colors. They are inexpensive to buy and easy to use, even for beginners. Cleanup is easy with soap and water.

◆ ACRYLIC PAINTING MEDIUMS

Blending gel medium is used with acrylic paints and gives a transparent look without changing the consistency of the paint. I like to use it when floating colors – I prefer it to **floating medium** because of its thicker consistency.

Latex glazing medium can be mixed with acrylic paint to extend the drying time of paint and provide textured and transparent effects.

Textile medium is mixed with acrylic paints so that the paints will adhere properly to fabric and be permanent.

◆ SEALERS & FINISHES

There are a variety of sealers and finishes available. They come in a variety of sheens – matte, satin, pearl, gloss, and high gloss, to name a few. Most of my projects are finished with a spray matte finish. Spray sealers are easy to apply and provide an even, consistent look. There are exterior brands of sealers available for projects that will be exposed to the elements. There are even sealers that have UV light protection to keep your colors from fading!

Choose a sealer that's compatible with the paint that you are using and that's appropriate for the way you will be using your piece and the look you want. Always follow the manufacturers' recommendations when applying their products.

◆ OTHER PAINTING SUPPLIES

A **whitewash stain and sealer** can be applied to unsealed wood and then wiped away, allowing the wood grain to show through. It provides a white-gray, transparent effect.

Use **decoupage medium** to adhere paper or fabric cutouts and embellishments to wood and other surfaces. The medium can be used as both glue and sealer. Look for it at crafts stores.

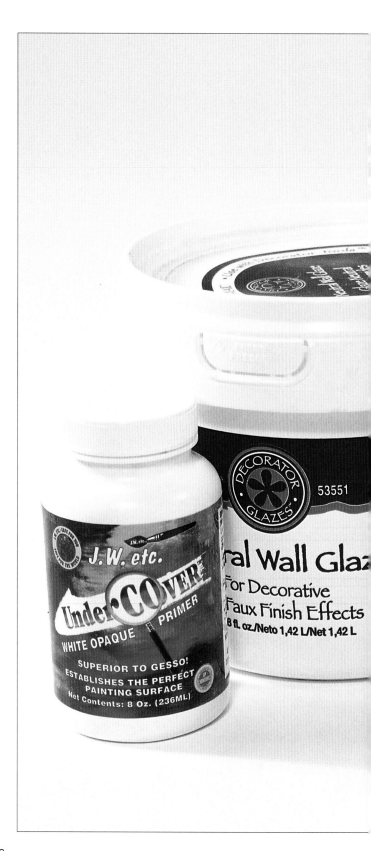

Pictured below: An assortment of primers, paints, sealers, and painting mediums. Look for them at crafts, paint, and hardware stores.

Artist's Paint Brushes

Good quality brushes are important – buy the best ones you can afford. I used the following brushes to paint the projects in this book:

Angular Brushes - 1/8", 1/4", 1/2", 3/4"
The angled brush is a flat edge brush that is cut at an angle. This brush is used to float or side-load. Dip the brush into water and remove the excess water on a paper towel. Dip the brush into blending gel and blend back & forth on the palette. Tip the longest edge of the brush into the paint and blend back & forth, working the paint into the bristles. The paint should remain predominately on one side of the brush, gradually blending to the other side. Angled brushed can also be used to walk out a float. (see Terms in Basic Information)

Liner Brushes - sizes 2, 4, 6
Liner brushes have shorter hairs than script liner brushes. Liner brushes are excellent for linework, outline designs, adding details and flowing lines for eyes, vines, flower centers, etc. It is recommended that when using a liner brush that the paint be thinned with water on the palette. Dip your brush into water and remove the excess water on a paper towel. Dip your brush into the thinned paint on your palette, slightly rolling it and pulling it towards you to load the brush. Hold the brush perpendicular to your painting surface and with light pressure paint your design or linework.

Script Liners - sizes 2/0, 0, 2, 4
The script liner is a long-haired round brush used for detail work such as scrolls, spirals and swirls. It is used with paint thinned with water on the palette. Dampen the brush in water and remove the excess on a paper towel. Roll the brush in the paint, pulling towards you, keeping the point on the brush. Keep the brush perpendicular to the surface, applying light pressure to paint the design.

Scruffy Brushes - sizes 0, 2, 4, 6, 8
Scruffy brushes are used to paint bushes, flower centers, backgrounds etc. It is not necessary to wet this brush prior to loading the paint. Load the brush by tipping it into the paint. Apply it to the surface with a pouncing or stippling motion. If more than one layer/color of paint is applied over a previously pounced area, leave some of the background showing through to give dimension to your painting.

Angular brushes of various sizes.

An assortment of liner brushes.

10

Square Wash - 1"

A wash brush is used for basecoating large areas, applying sealers or slip-slap blending (see Terms in Basic Information). Dip the brush in water and remove the excess on a paper towel. Dip the brush into the paint, blend into the bristles and paint the desired areas on your design.

Round Brushes - sizes 2, 4, 6, 8, 10

(Combination 50/50 of natural & synthetic hair). Round brushes have a round ferrule with hairs that come to a point. Round brushes are good for basecoating, painting details, & small areas such as tips on leaves, hearts, etc. Dampen the brush in water and remove the excess water on a paper towel. Dip the tip of the brush into the paint.

Filbert - size 8

The filbert brush is a flat brush with a rounded or curved end. It is used for flower petals (hydrangea) and leaves. It can also be used for filling in and blending. Dip the brush into the water and remove excess on a paper towel. Dip the tip of the brush into the paint bending it on the palette so that the paint will be pulled up into the bristles. Apply pressure to the brush when on your surface and slightly lift the brush as you pull it towards you. As you are slowly pulling the brush towards you, turn the brush 90º and raise it to its chisel edge. This will give you the point at the end of your petal or tip of your leaf.

Brights (Flat) sizes 6 & 10

Brights are rectangular shaped brushes that have a chisel edge. They are used for basecoating, wide stripes, and stroke leaves. For a stroke leaf, dip your brush into water and remove the excess on a paper towel. Dip the brush into paint on the palette and blend the paint onto the bristles by stroking the brush back and forth. Apply pressure to the brush as you paint on your surface. As you pull the brush towards you slowly, turn it 90º and raise it to its chisel edge. Stroke leaves may be painted with a double-loaded brush. (see painting terms)

Interlocked Hog-Bristled Brushes (Round-short) - sizes 4, 6, 8

These coarse brushes are used for "dry-brushing" (see Terms in Basic Information). It is not necessary to wet the brush prior to painting this technique. Dry-brushing gives an illusion of dimension to the painted surfaces. Dry-brushing can be used for highlighting areas such as cheeks, flower centers, petals, fruit and leaves.

Wash brush (top) and Scruffy brushes.

Round brushes (top five) and Interlocked Hog-Bristle brushes

Other Painting Tools

It's always good to have a few 3" to 4" **foam rollers** and **foam brushes** on hand for base painting larger areas. Using them saves wear and tear on your smaller brushes.

I like **Sea sponges** for creating textures. A glaze brush, which has short, natural bristles, is used to apply brush-on varnishes.

Pictured left to right: Sea sponge, glaze brush, foam brushes, foam roller.

Miscellaneous Basic Supplies

FOR TRANSFERRING DESIGNS

Transfer paper is a thin paper that is coated on one side with chalk or graphite that's used for transferring designs. It comes in a variety of brands, colors, and sizes and can be purchased in large sheets, rolls, and smaller packages that have an assortment of colors.

I prefer the kind of transfer paper with lines that can be removed with water instead of an eraser. I use a **kneaded eraser** for removing lines left by carbon and graphite transfer paper.

A **stylus** is a tool with a small rounded tip that is used to transfer designs using transfer paper.

Use **tracing paper** to trace patterns from the book.

FOR SANDING

I use **400 grit sandpaper** for sanding and a **tack cloth** to remove sanding dust and particles. A tack cloth is usually made of cheesecloth and is slightly sticky.

FOR PAINTING

You'll need a **water basin** for rinsing brushes, **paper towels** for blotting, a **wet palette** for holding paints, and a **paper palette** for blending colors.

BASIC
INFORMATION

Preparing Surfaces

Old Wood

It's important to properly prepare old wood surfaces, such as previously painted pieces or recycled furniture.

Here's how:

1. Remove all grease and dirt residue. Wipe with mineral spirits or paint thinner, if necessary. Wipe away any residue with a cotton rag.

2. Sand with fine sandpaper. Sanding creates a "tooth" so paint will adhere to the surface.

3. Wipe with a tack cloth.

4. Apply a good coat of primer. Primer prevents old paint, stains, and imperfections from seeping through your new design. Primer also increases paint adhesion.

Sanding with fine grit sandpaper.

New Wood

New wood surfaces need less in the way of preparation.

1. Lightly sand.

2. Wipe with a tack cloth to remove dust.

3. Apply one thin coat of wood sealer. Let dry completely.

4. If the wood grain is raised after sealing, sand again with very fine sandpaper (400 grit). Remove all dust.

Fabric

Acrylic paints work well on fabric surfaces, including canvas. Before you begin to paint, mix textile medium with the paint colors you will be using. Follow the textile medium manufacturer's instructions regarding the ratio of paint to medium.

Applying primer with a foam brush.

Terms

BASE PAINT

This is an even smooth undercoat or first coat of paint that is applied to the painting surface, usually prior to the pattern being transferred. Sometimes two coats of the base paint are required for adequate coverage.

BASECOAT

This is the first coat of paint applied to an element of the design.

DRY BRUSH

For this technique, use a hog-bristled coarse round brush and don't dampen the brush prior to painting. Dip the brush in the un-thinned paint. Blend and slightly scrub the paint into the bristles. Rub the brush in a circular motion on a paper towel until hardly any paint remains – only a hint of paint should be coming off of the brush. Swirl the brush lightly on the surface while applying pressure. The result should be a soft, shaded look.

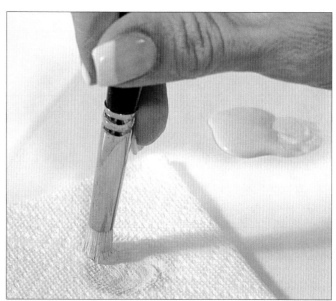

Rubbing off paint on a paper towel.

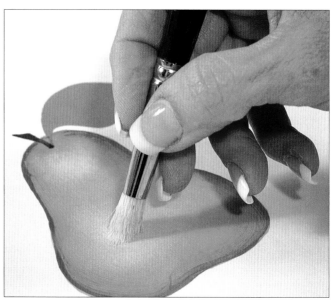

Dry brushing with a swirling motion.

FLOATING

Floating is done with a sideloaded brush – you load paint on one side of the brush and a medium on the other side. The medium can be water, floating medium, or blending gel medium. I prefer to use angular brushes for floating.

Here's how:

1. Dip your brush in water. Remove the excess water by blotting the brush on a paper towel.

2. Dip the brush in your chosen medium and stroke back and forth on your palette.

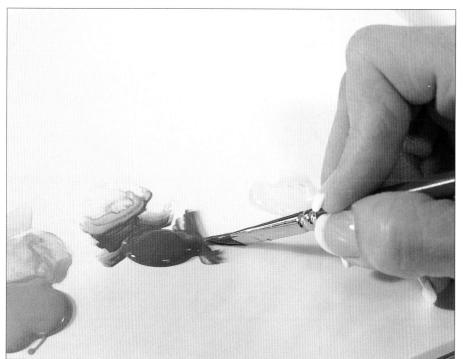

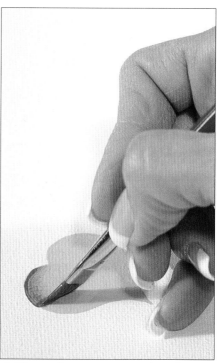

3. Dip one side of the brush (the long tip of an angular brush) in paint. This is called "sideloading." Stroke back and forth on the palette to blend. The paint should gradually fade from strong (on one side of the brush) to barely visible (on the other side).

4. Float the paint on the design, placing the side of the brush that was sideloaded with the paint color on the outer edge.

SLIP-SLAP BLENDING

In this technique, you apply two (or more) paint colors to a surface by moving the brush in an irregular, loose back-and-forth (sometimes diagonal) stroking motion. The colors are mingled, but not completely or uniformly blended.

1. Applying the first color.

2. Applying the second color.

WALKING OUT A FLOAT

For this technique, begin by floating paint on an area. Gradually blend the color, "walking" the brush away from the original floated area. The color should fade from strong to light.

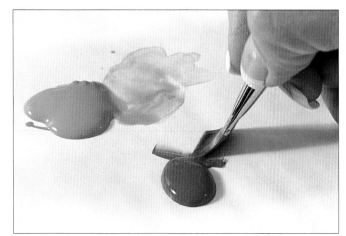

1. Sideloading a brush with paint.

2. Placing the float.

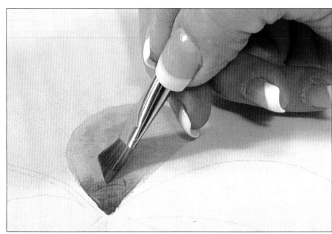

3. Walking the brush out to blend and fade the color.

WASH

A wash looks transparent when brushed on – the background or base color should show through.

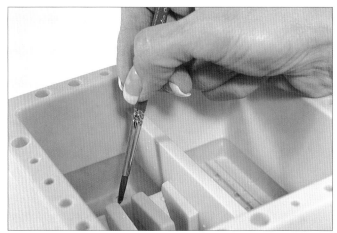

Dipping the brush in water.

Mixing water with paint to thin the paint and achieve an inky consistency.

Applying a wash of thinned paint.

Transferring Patterns

Patterns are included for all the designs. Use tracing paper and a pencil to trace the design from the book. Enlarge or reduce as needed (it's handy to use a photocopier) to fit your surface. Use transfer paper and a stylus to transfer the design to the surface.

Using the Painting Worksheets

This book includes numerous painting worksheets that accompany the projects and illustrate the painting techniques, design motifs, and details of the designs. Refer to them for guidance as you paint. You can also use them as springboards for creating your own designs from the various motifs for new looks or coordinated pieces.

PROJECTS

his section contains 20 fun, simple-to-paint projects for furniture and accessories that will add color, pattern, and interest to indoor and outdoor rooms. Many are suitable for use outdoors; all of them can be used on a covered porch or patio.

An assortment of surfaces – wood, metal, glass, fabric, and papier mache – are represented. The designs can be adapted to fit a variety of furniture pieces and for multiple uses. Use them as they are presented for beautiful, proven results or adapt the ideas, techniques, and motifs to create your own inspired treasures, choosing surfaces and colors that work with your decor.

All of the projects include a list of supplies you'll need, including paint colors, brushes, and finishes. For each project, in addition to the supplies listed, **you'll need a few basic supplies:**

• **Tracing paper and pencil or pen,** for tracing patterns from the book

• **Transfer paper and stylus,** for transferring the design to the project surface

• **Sandpaper,** for smoothing wood

• **Wood sealer,** for sealing new wood surfaces

FRUITS OF THE SEASON
drop leaf table

This table was a new, unfinished piece, but the design could be adapted to a variety of furniture pieces. To help you get started, step-by-step photos of the painting techniques are included.

COLOR PALETTE

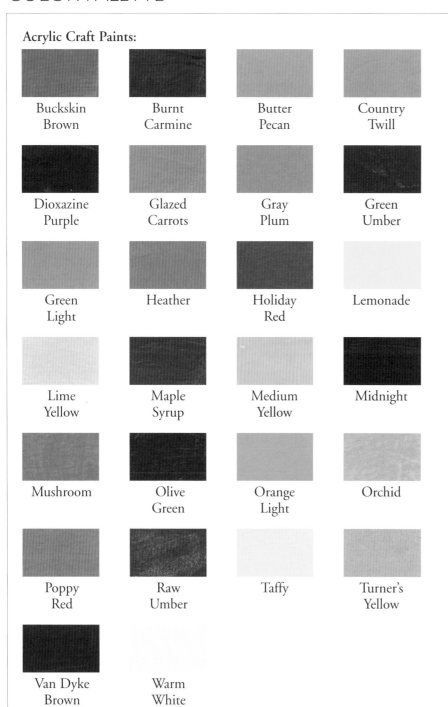

Acrylic Craft Paints:

Buckskin Brown

Burnt Carmine

Butter Pecan

Country Twill

Dioxazine Purple

Glazed Carrots

Gray Plum

Green Umber

Green Light

Heather

Holiday Red

Lemonade

Lime Yellow

Maple Syrup

Medium Yellow

Midnight

Mushroom

Olive Green

Orange Light

Orchid

Poppy Red

Raw Umber

Taffy

Turner's Yellow

Van Dyke Brown

Warm White

SURFACE
Wooden drop leaf table with lower shelf (Top is 18" x 19".)

BRUSHES
Rounds - sizes 4, 6, 8, 10
Angulars - 1/8", 1/4", 3/4"
Liners - sizes 2, 4, 6
Square Wash - 1"
Script liners - 2/0, 2
Interlocked Hog-Bristled (Round-short) - sizes 4, 6, 8

OTHER SUPPLIES
Exterior satin sealer
Blending gel medium

PREPARE SURFACE
1. Sand table. Wipe away dust.
2. Apply sealer. Let dry.
3. Base paint the base and sides of the table with Butter Pecan.
4. Base paint the top of the table with Mushroom. Let dry.
5. Transfer the design.

continued on page 22

20

PAINT THE DESIGN

Border & Vines:

1. Paint the border on the top of the table with Taffy.
2. Paint the vines around the border and in between the fruits and the stems with Van Dyke Brown.
3. Just next to the edges of the vines, paint a thin line of Maple Syrup.
4. In the centers of the vines, paint thin lines of Country Twill.

Pears:

Also see the Pear Worksheet.

1. Basecoat the pears with Turner's Yellow.
2. Basecoat the stems with Van Dyke Brown.

3. Load brush with blending gel medium.

4. Sideload brush with Buckskin Brown.

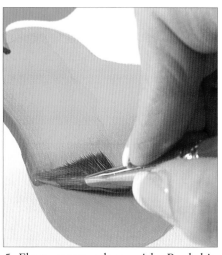

5. Float outer edges with Buckskin Brown. See Pear Worksheet, Fig. 1. Let dry.

6. Roll brush into Lemonade.

7. Rub off paint on a paper towel.

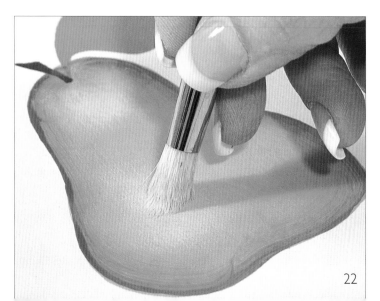

8. Dry brush the highlight areas with Lemonade. See Pear Worksheet, Fig. 2.

9. Float the indentation at the base of the stem with Burnt Carmine.

10. Highlight stem with Maple Syrup, then Country Twill. See the Pear Worksheet, Fig. 2.

Instructions continue on page 24

Pear Worksheet

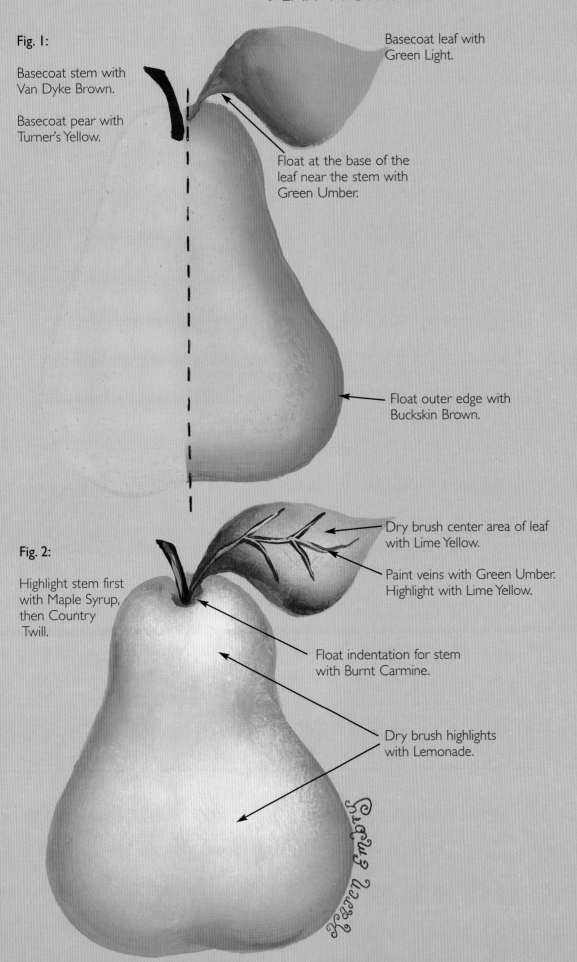

Fig. 1:

Basecoat stem with Van Dyke Brown.

Basecoat pear with Turner's Yellow.

Basecoat leaf with Green Light.

Float at the base of the leaf near the stem with Green Umber.

Float outer edge with Buckskin Brown.

Fig. 2:

Highlight stem first with Maple Syrup, then Country Twill.

Dry brush center area of leaf with Lime Yellow.

Paint veins with Green Umber. Highlight with Lime Yellow.

Float indentation for stem with Burnt Carmine.

Dry brush highlights with Lemonade.

Karen Embry

continued from page 22

Grapes:

Also see the Grape & Plum Worksheet that follows these instructions.

1. Basecoat grapes with Heather.

2. Basecoat stem of cluster with Van Dyke Brown.

3. Paint the dark spaces in between the grapes with Dioxazine Purple.

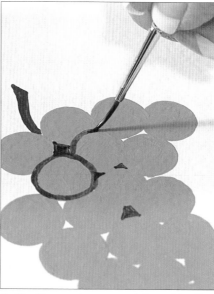

4. Outline each grape with a thin line of thinned Dioxazine Purple.

5. Mix equal amounts of Dioxazine Purple and Burnt Carmine on your palette.

6. Float the bottoms of the grapes with the Dioxazine Purple/Burnt Carmine mix.

7. Mix equal amounts of Heather and Warm White. Float the tops of the grapes with the Heather/Warm White mix.

8. Dry brush the tops of the grapes with the Heather/Warm White mix.

9. Paint tiny highlights on grapes with Warm White.

Instructions continue on page 26

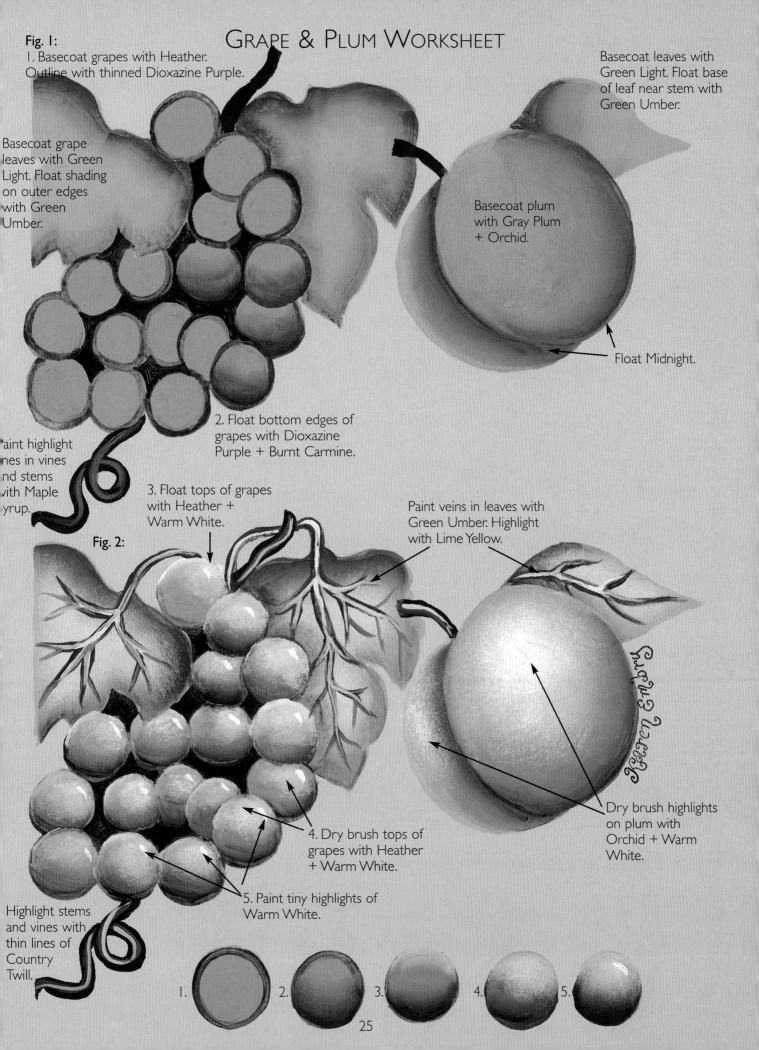

GRAPE & PLUM WORKSHEET

Fig. 1:
1. Basecoat grapes with Heather. Outline with thinned Dioxazine Purple.

Basecoat grape leaves with Green Light. Float shading on outer edges with Green Umber.

Basecoat leaves with Green Light. Float base of leaf near stem with Green Umber.

Basecoat plum with Gray Plum + Orchid.

Float Midnight.

Paint highlight lines in vines and stems with Maple Syrup.

2. Float bottom edges of grapes with Dioxazine Purple + Burnt Carmine.

3. Float tops of grapes with Heather + Warm White.

Paint veins in leaves with Green Umber. Highlight with Lime Yellow.

Fig. 2:

4. Dry brush tops of grapes with Heather + Warm White.

Dry brush highlights on plum with Orchid + Warm White.

5. Paint tiny highlights of Warm White.

Highlight stems and vines with thin lines of Country Twill.

1.   2.   3.   4.   5.

25

continued from page 24

Apples:

See the Apple & Peach Worksheet that follows these instructions.

1. Basecoat apples with Holiday Red.
2. Basecoat the stem with Van Dyke Brown.
3. Float outer edges of the apple with Burnt Carmine.
4. Dry brush highlight areas with Poppy Red. Let dry. See the Apple & Pear Worksheet, Fig. 1.
5. Dry brush highlight areas with Medium Yellow. See the Apple & Pear Worksheet, Fig. 2. Let dry.
6. Dry brush highlight areas with Turner's Yellow. See the Apple & Pear Worksheet, Fig. 2.
7. Float the indentation at the base of the stem with Burnt Carmine.
8. Highlight the stems first with Maple Syrup, then Country Twill.

Plums:

See the Grape & Plum Worksheet that follows these instructions.

1. Mix equal amounts Gray Plum and Orchid. Basecoat plums.
2. Basecoat stems with Van Dyke Brown.
3. Float bottom edges of plums and the splits in the plums with Midnight.
4. Mix equal amounts Orchid and Warm White. Dry brush highlights.
5. Highlight the stems first with Maple Syrup, then Country Twill.

Peaches:

See the Apple & Peach Worksheet that follows these instructions.

1. Basecoat peach with Orange Light.
2. Basecoat stem with Van Dyke Brown.
3. Mix equal amounts Buckskin Brown and Glazed Carrots. Float shading on right side of peach and the split in the peach with the mix.
4. Dry brush highlight areas with Turner's Yellow. Let dry. See the Apple & Peach Worksheet, Fig. 2.
5. Dry brush highlight areas with Lemonade.
6. Highlight the stem first with Maple Syrup, then Country Twill.

APPLE & PEACH WORKSHEET

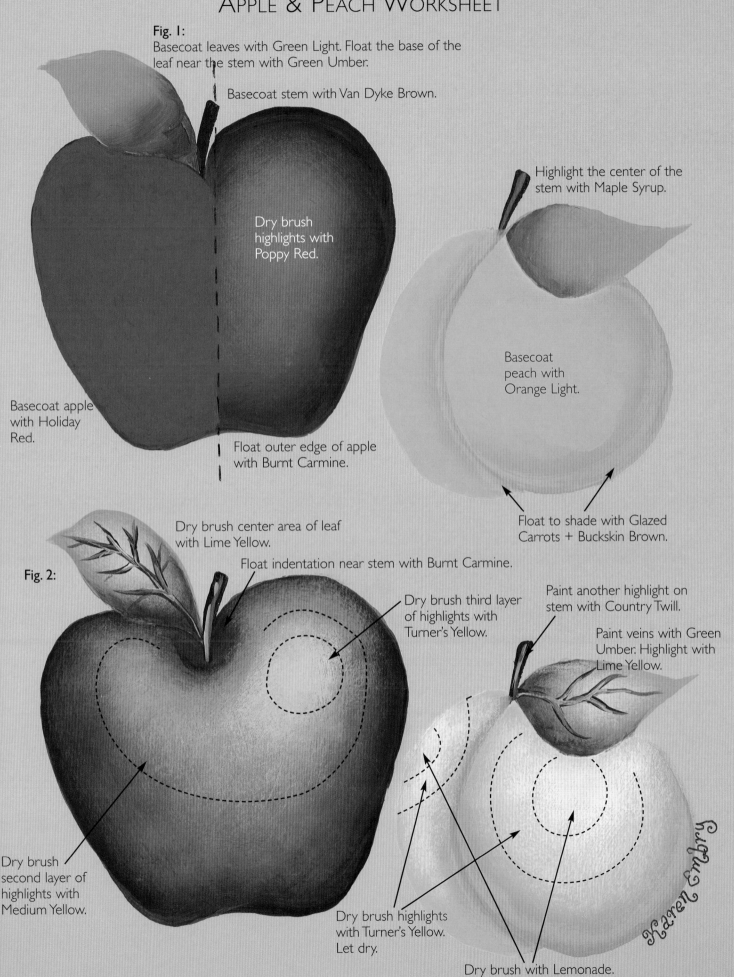

Fig. 1:
Basecoat leaves with Green Light. Float the base of the leaf near the stem with Green Umber.

Basecoat stem with Van Dyke Brown.

Highlight the center of the stem with Maple Syrup.

Dry brush highlights with Poppy Red.

Basecoat peach with Orange Light.

Basecoat apple with Holiday Red.

Float outer edge of apple with Burnt Carmine.

Float to shade with Glazed Carrots + Buckskin Brown.

Dry brush center area of leaf with Lime Yellow.

Float indentation near stem with Burnt Carmine.

Fig. 2:

Dry brush third layer of highlights with Turner's Yellow.

Paint another highlight on stem with Country Twill.

Paint veins with Green Umber. Highlight with Lime Yellow.

Dry brush second layer of highlights with Medium Yellow.

Dry brush highlights with Turner's Yellow. Let dry.

Dry brush with Lemonade.

Karen Embry

27

continued from page 26

Leaves:

All of the leaves are painted the same way. You can paint the leaves as you complete each fruit or paint all the leaves at one time. The photos in this section use the pear leaf as an example.

1. Basecoat with Green Light.

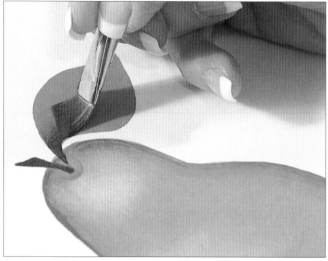

2. Float shading on the stem end with Green Umber.

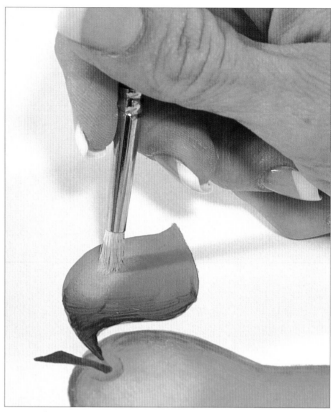

3. Dry brush the centers of the leaves with Lime Yellow.

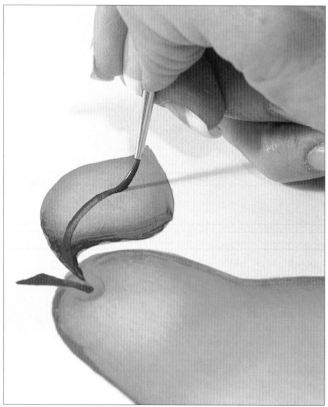

4. Paint veins with Green Umber.

5. Highlight veins with Lime Yellow.

FINISH

1. Float around edges of all leaves and fruits with Raw Umber. Let dry.

2. Apply two coats of exterior satin sealer. ❑

Pattern for Fruits of the Season Drop Leaf Table
Enlarge @220% for actual size.

QUEEN OF HEARTS
bentwood chair

This chair was a flea market find, but the design can be enlarged or reduced to accommodate the size of your chair or another painting surface.

COLOR PALETTE

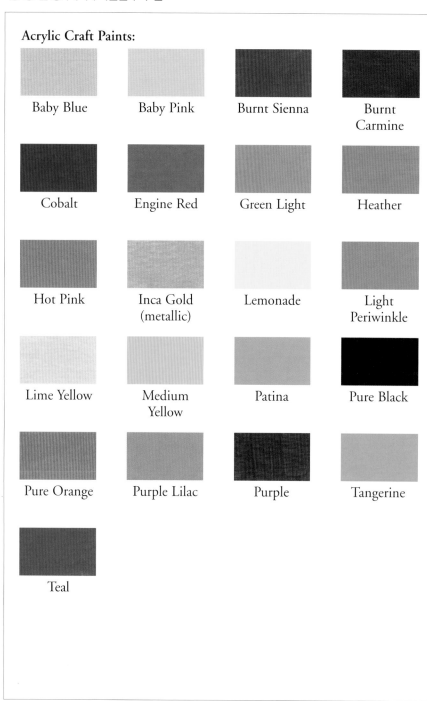

Acrylic Craft Paints:

Baby Blue · Baby Pink · Burnt Sienna · Burnt Carmine

Cobalt · Engine Red · Green Light · Heather

Hot Pink · Inca Gold (metallic) · Lemonade · Light Periwinkle

Lime Yellow · Medium Yellow · Patina · Pure Black

Pure Orange · Purple Lilac · Purple · Tangerine

Teal

SURFACE
Bentwood chair

BRUSHES
Brights - sizes 6, 8
Angulars - 1/4", 3/4"
Script Liners - sizes 2/0, 2
Rounds - sizes 4, 6
Square Wash - 1"

OTHER SUPPLIES
Exterior sealer

PREPARE SURFACE
1. Prepare chair for painting, following the recommendations for previously painted furniture in the Basic Instructions section of this book.
2. Mix equal amounts Heather and Light Periwinkle. Base paint the chair with the mix. Let dry.
3. Transfer the design.

PAINT THE DESIGN
See the Hearts Worksheet for examples of basecoats, shading, and details.
Basecoats:
1. Basecoat the crown, the stripes between the hearts on the chair back, and edge of the seat with Inca Gold.
2. Paint the five hearts at the top of the crown with these colors (from left to right): Engine Red, Lime Yellow, Baby Pink, Patina, and Tangerine.

continued on page 33

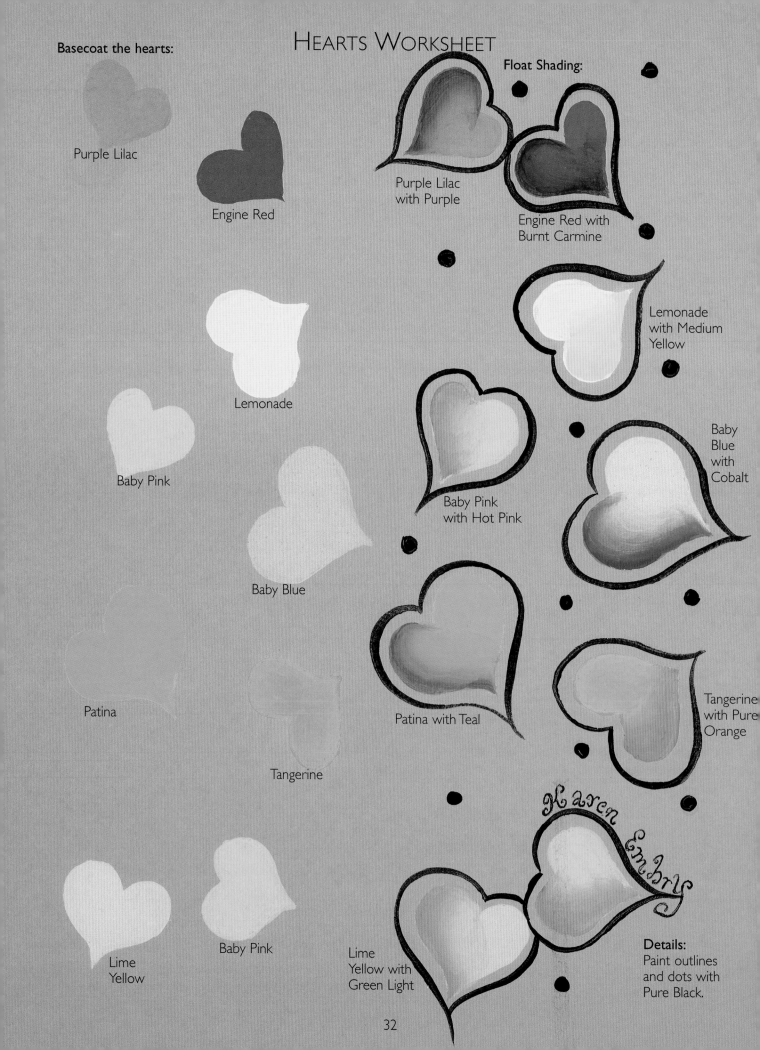

HEARTS WORKSHEET

Basecoat the hearts:

Purple Lilac

Engine Red

Lemonade

Baby Pink

Baby Blue

Patina

Tangerine

Lime Yellow

Baby Pink

Float Shading:

Purple Lilac with Purple

Engine Red with Burnt Carmine

Lemonade with Medium Yellow

Baby Pink with Hot Pink

Baby Blue with Cobalt

Patina with Teal

Tangerine with Pure Orange

Lime Yellow with Green Light

Karen Embry

Details:
Paint outlines and dots with Pure Black.

32

continued from page 30

3. Basecoat the eight hearts on the chair seat with these colors, beginning at the heart at center back: Baby Pink, Lemonade, Patina, Engine Red, Tangerine, Baby Blue, Purple Lilac, and Lime Yellow.

4. Basecoat the hearts on the chair back with these colors, top to bottom: Baby Pink, Patina, Tangerine, Engine Red and Lemonade.

5. Paint hearts randomly on the chair legs, alternating colors.

Shading:

1. Float the bottom of the crown with Burnt Sienna.

2. Float one side of the Baby Pink hearts with Hot Pink.

3. Float one side of the Lemonade hearts with Medium Yellow.

4. Float one the side of the Engine Red hearts with Burnt Carmine.

5. Float one side of the Tangerine hearts with Pure Orange.

6. Float one side of the Baby Blue hearts with Cobalt.

7. Float one side of the Purple Lilac hearts with Purple.

8. Float one side of the Lime Yellow hearts with Green Light.

9. Float one side of the Patina hearts with Teal.

Details:

Paint the lettering, outlines, and dots with Pure Black. Let dry completely.

FINISH

Apply two coats of exterior sealer. Let the sealer dry between coats. ❏

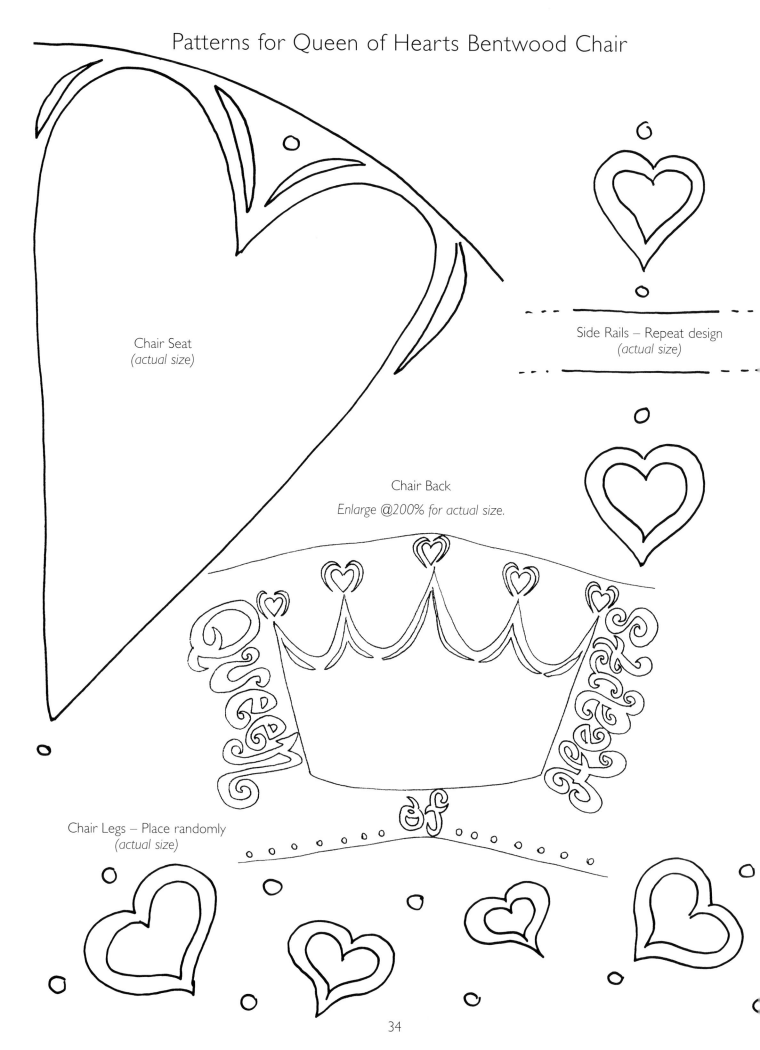

Patterns for Queen of Hearts Bentwood Chair

Chair Seat
(actual size)

Side Rails – Repeat design
(actual size)

Chair Back

Enlarge @200% for actual size.

Chair Legs – Place randomly
(actual size)

Pattern for Words to Live By Garden Bench
(See page 40 for additional patterns for this project.)
(actual size)

WORDS TO LIVE BY
garden bench

This garden bench is a new, unfinished piece with a removable oval panel in the back.
(If your bench has a plain back, you can mask off an oval and paint it the same way. The
petal flowers and vines are painted; the other motifs and words are stenciled. You can use
pre-cut stencils or cut your own, using the patterns provided.
The amethyst glass curtain rod finials and the glass bead fringe look beautiful in sunlight.
(If you're planning to keep the bench outdoors, don't use the bead fringe –
the glue and ribbon won't hold up in weather.)

COLOR PALETTE

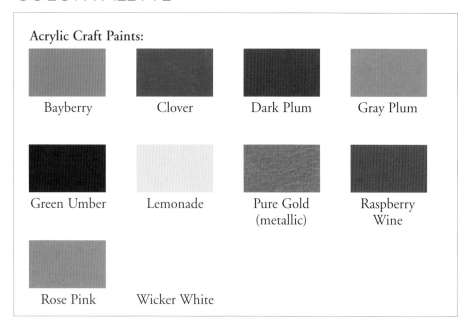

Acrylic Craft Paints:

Bayberry

Clover

Dark Plum

Gray Plum

Green Umber

Lemonade

Pure Gold
(metallic)

Raspberry
Wine

Rose Pink

Wicker White

SURFACE
Wooden garden bench, 34" tall, 5 ft.
long, 32" deep

BRUSHES
Brights - sizes 6, 8
Angulars - 1/4", 3/4"
Script Liners - sizes 2/0, 2
Rounds - sizes 4, 6
Square Wash - 1"

OTHER SUPPLIES
Painter's masking tape, 1" wide

Paper doily, 14" x 10"

2 curtain rod finials with screws on
the ends

Sea sponge

Glazing medium

Sectioned foam plate

2 pieces of glass bead fringe on a
ribbon, each 3-1/2 ft. long

Thick white glue

Decoupage medium

Pre-cut stencils - hearts, flowers, sun,
stars, diamond border, alphabets *or*
stencil blank material, fine tip
marker, and craft knife

Exterior varnish

PREPARE SURFACE
1. Remove the oval panel. Sand bench and panel. Wipe away dust.
2. Seal bench and panel. Let dry.
3. Base paint back, top, seat, panel and outer sides of bench with Wicker White.
4. Basecoat the inside of the arm rests/sides with Lemonade. Let dry.
5. Transfer the patterns. Arrange them randomly as shown on photo.
6. Mask off the stripes on the back and the seat with painter's tape.

PAINT THE DESIGN
See "How to Sponge on page 38."
Sponging:
1. On a sectioned foam plate, squeeze puddles of three colors: Rose Pink, Gray Plum,
   and Bayberry. Mix four parts glazing medium with each color. Dampen the sea
   sponge and squeeze out excess water.
2. Sponge the oval panel with the pink glaze mixture, applying the glaze more heavily on
   the edges and fading out toward the center. Rinse sponge and squeeze out excess water.

Continued on page 38

continued from page 36

3. Sponge the panel with the plum glaze mixture. Take care not to muddy the colors. The effect should be light and transparent. Rinse sponge and squeeze out excess water.
4. Sponge the oval again with the green glaze mixture, concentrating the color on the edges and fading out toward the center.

Stripes:
1. Basecoat the outer stripe on each side with Gray Plum.
2. Float the outer edges of these stripes with Dark Plum.
3. Basecoat the inner stripe on each side with Rose Pink.
4. Float the outer edges of each of these stripes with Raspberry Wine.

Diamonds:
Basecoat the diamonds on the outer side sections with Gray Plum.

Seat:
1. Basecoat the center rectangular of the seat with Bayberry.
2. Float outer edges of the rectangle with Clover.
3. Paint the vines and leaves with Green Umber.
4. Using decoupage medium, glue the doily to the seat, using the photo as a guide for placement. Let dry.
5. Apply a coat of decoupage medium over the doily. Let dry.

Flowers:
See the Garden Flowers Worksheet.
1. Basecoat all the flower petals with Rose Pink.
2. Basecoat the centers with Raspberry Wine.
3. Float the edges of the petals with Raspberry Wine.
4. Paint the lines coming from the centers of the flowers to the petals with Raspberry Wine.
5. Paint the linework details on the petals with Wicker White.
6. Paint Lemonade highlights in the center of each flower.

Embellishments:
1. Using the photo as a guide for placement, stencil the words "BELIEVE", "Love", "Imagine," "Dream", and "HOPE" with colors of your choice from the palette for this project.
2. Stencil hearts, stars, stylized flowers, and suns in various colors.
3. Stencil the diamonds-and-bars border along the bottom of the seat back.

Trim:
1. Paint the top edge of the back and the top edges of the arms with Pure Gold .
2. Mask off the gold trim stripes at the bottom of the back and along the front edge of the seat. Paint with Pure Gold . Remove tape and let dry.

FINISH
1. Insert the panel in the bench back.
2. Apply two coats of exterior satin sealer, letting the sealer dry between coats.
3. Screw the finials in the top corners of the bench.
4. Glue the bead fringe to the lower backrest section of the chair and the lower part of the front of the seat. ❏

How to Sponge
Sponging adds a wonderful mottled look to your background, giving it more interest and a textured look. It is easy to do and offers a big payoff.

You Will Need:
Acrylic paint colors; Sea Sponge; Glazing Medium; Palette

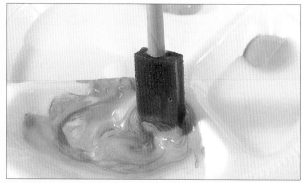

1. Mix paint with glazing medium (one part paint to four parts glazing medium). A partitioned foam plate makes a good palette for this project.

2. Dampen a sea sponge and squeeze out excess water. Dip in the pink glaze mixture. Pounce the sponge on the surface, creating texture. Vary the position of the sponge as you work.

3. Pick up the second color on the sponge and pounce, then the third.

GARDEN FLOWERS WORKSHEET

Fig. 1:

Paint vines and leaves with Green Umber.

Basecoat flower petals with Rose Pink. Paint flower centers with Raspberry Wine.

Fig. 2:

Float the edges of the petals with Raspberry Wine.

Fig. 3:

Paint linework details of petals with Wicker White.

Paint lines on the petals from the centers with Raspberry Wine.

Paint highlights in flower centers with Lemonade.

Karen Embry

39

Pattern for Words to Live By Garden Bench

Additional patterns appear on page 35

(actual size)

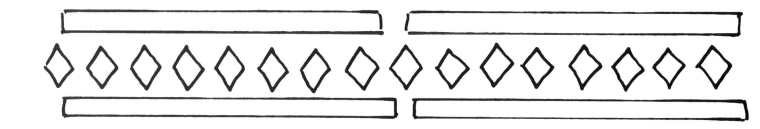

Diamond Pattern
Repeat to cover sides.
(actual size)

FAIREST OF THEM ALL
mirror

Fit for the bedroom of a princess, this mirror is painted with fanciful flora and fauna and adorned with rhinestones. Removing the mirror from the frame makes the painting much easier.

COLOR PALETTE

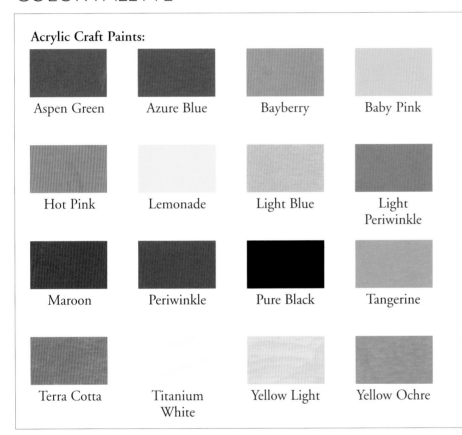

Acrylic Craft Paints:

Aspen Green

Azure Blue

Bayberry

Baby Pink

Hot Pink

Lemonade

Light Blue

Light Periwinkle

Maroon

Periwinkle

Pure Black

Tangerine

Terra Cotta

Titanium White

Yellow Light

Yellow Ochre

SURFACE
Arch-top wood frame mirror

BRUSHES
Angular - 1/4"

Liners - sizes 2, 4

Bright - size 6

Round - size 4

OTHER SUPPLIES
Assorted small rhinestones

White craft glue

Matte sealer spray

PREPARE SURFACE
1. Sand frame. Remove dust.
2. Seal the surface. Let dry.
3. Basecoat the frame with Lemonade. Let dry.
4. Transfer the design.

PAINT THE DESIGN
See the Heart & Bluebird Worksheet.

Vines & Leaves:
1. Paint the vines with Bayberry.
2. Paint a thin line right next to the vine with Aspen Green.
3. Basecoat one half of each leaf with Aspen Green. Basecoat the other half with Bayberry.

Hearts:
1. Basecoat the outer part of both hearts with Maroon.
2. Basecoat the middle section of the hearts with Hot Pink.
3. Basecoat the centers of the hearts with Baby Pink.
4. Paint dots on hearts with Wicker White.

Roses:
1. Basecoat with Hot Pink.
2. Float the outer edges with Maroon.
3. Paint the circular swirls in the roses with Baby Pink.

Bird:
1. Basecoat with Periwinkle.
2. Basecoat the inner area of the bird with Light Periwinkle.
3. Paint the beak with Yellow Ochre.
4. Paint eye with Wicker White.
5. Dot the pupil with Pure Black.

Petaled Flowers:
1. Basecoat the flower petals with Yellow Light.
2. Outline the petals with Yellow Ochre.
3. Paint the flower centers with Terra Cotta.
4. Highlight the flower centers with Tangerine.

continued on page 45

Heart & Bluebird Worksheet

Paint the wings with Azure Blue and the center of the wings with Light Blue. Paint antennae and body with Black.

Basecoat heart:

Maroon

Hot Pink

Baby Pink

Paint vines with Bayberry. Paint leaves with half Bayberry, half Aspen Green.

Basecoat roses with Hot Pink. Float Maroon around outer edges.

Paint bird with Periwinkle, then Light Periwinkle.

Paint highlight details with Periwinkle. Dot top edges with Wicker White.

Add dots on leaves with Wicker White.

Swirl Baby Pink in centers.

Add detail lines on hearts and bird with Pure Black.

continued from page 43

Big Butterfly:
1. Paint the wings with Azure Blue.
2. Paint the body and antennae with Pure Black.
3. Paint the centers of the wings with Light Blue.
4. Paint the highlight details on the wings with Periwinkle.
5. Dot upper edges of wings with Wicker White.

Small Butterflies:
1. Paint wings with Periwinkle.
2. Dot wings with Wicker White.

Trim:
1. Paint checks around top of mirror, at bottom, and around center area of mirror with Pure Black and Wicker White.
2. Paint lettering, lines of dots, and linework around flowers, bird, hearts, and leaves with Pure Black.
3. Paint trios of dots near leaves and hearts with Wicker White. Let dry completely.

FINISH

1. Spray with two coats of matte sealer.
2. Re-install mirror in frame.
3. Glue on an assortment of small rhinestones. ❏

Patterns for Mirror
Enlarge @220% for actual size.

HOME IS WHERE YOU HANG YOUR HEART

wall shelf

A simple ivy leaf design adorns this wooden shelf. Use it outside for tools or inside for keys or coats.

COLOR PALETTE

Acrylic Craft Paints:

Bayberry

Burnt Umber

Linen

Olive Green

Wicker White

SURFACE

Wooden shelf with hooks, 29" wide

BRUSHES

Liners - sizes 2, 4

Angulars - 1/4" 1/2"

Rounds - sizes 4, 6

Script Liner - size 2/0

OTHER SUPPLIES

Matte sealer spray

PREPARE SURFACE

1. Remove hooks.
2. Lightly sand wood and wipe away any dust.
3. Apply one coat of wood sealer. Let dry.
4. Basecoat shelf with two coats of Linen, letting dry between coats.
5. Transfer the design.

PAINT THE DESIGN

See the Ivy Leaf Worksheet.

Ivy Leaves & Vines:

1. Basecoat the leaves with Bayberry.
2. Basecoat the vines with Olive Green.
3. Float the bottom edges of the leaves with Olive Green.
4. Paint highlight lines on the vines with Bayberry.
5. Float the top edges of the leaves and just below the center veins with Wicker White.
6. Paint the veins in the leaves with Olive Green.

Lettering & Trim:

1. Mix equal amounts of Burnt Umber and Olive Green. Paint the lettering.
2. Float around the outside edges of the leaves with Burnt Umber.
3. Paint the edge of the shelf with Bayberry. Let dry.

FINISH

1. Spray with two lights coats of matte sealer. Let dry.
2. Re-attach the hooks. ❑

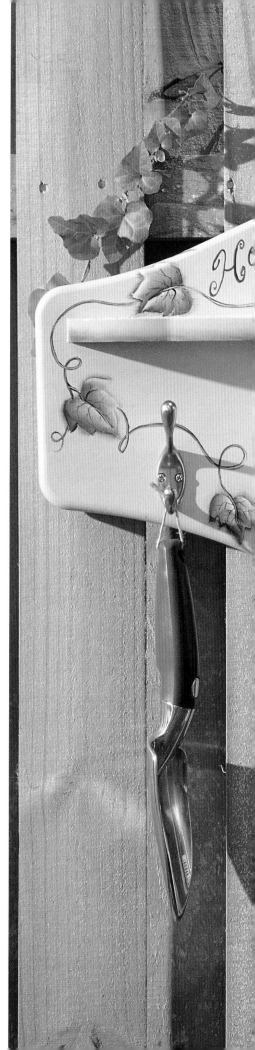

Ivy Leaf Worksheet

Basecoat leaves with Bayberry.
Basecoat vines with Olive Green.

Float the bottom edges of the
leaves with Olive Green.

Float the top edges of the leaves
and just below the center veins
with Wicker White.

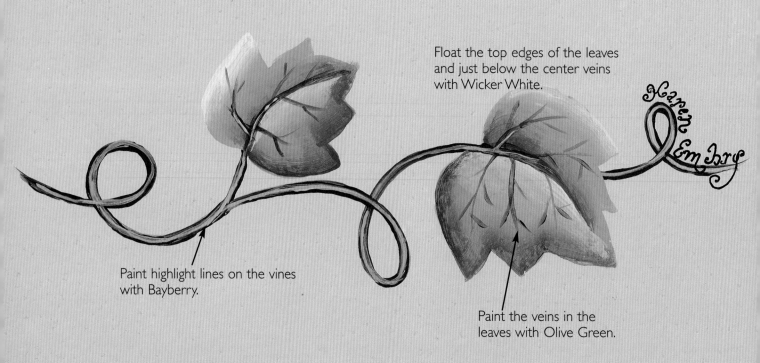

Paint highlight lines on the vines
with Bayberry.

Paint the veins in the
leaves with Olive Green.

Pattern for Wall Shelf
Enlarge @ 250% for actual size.

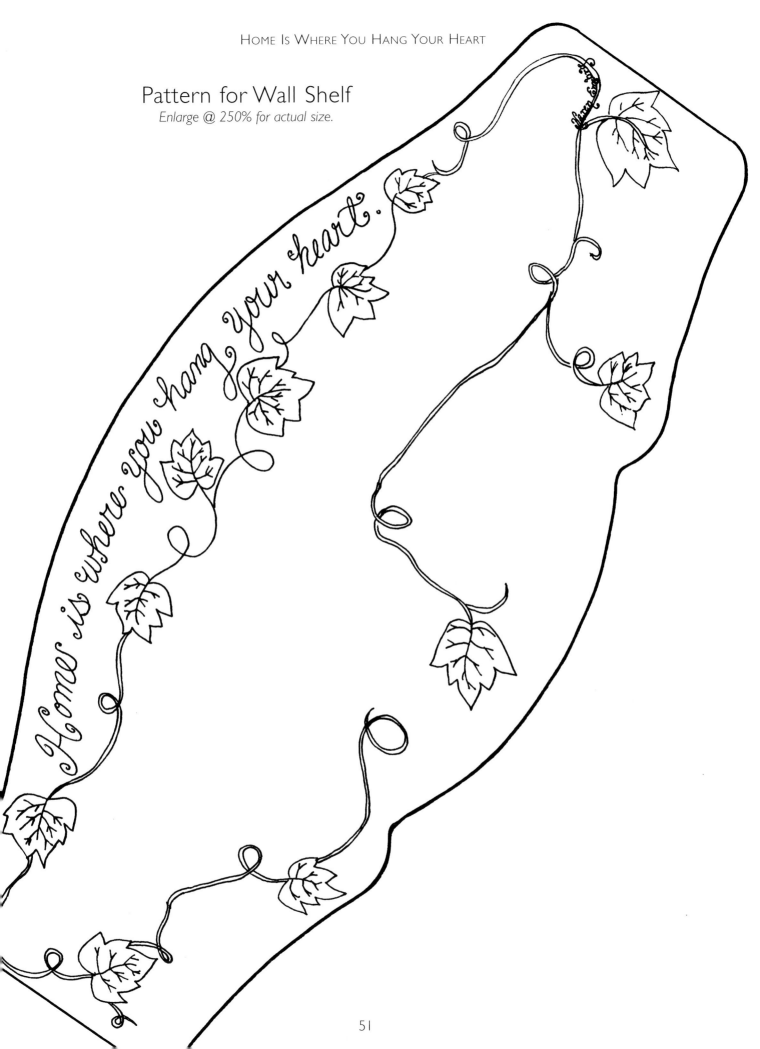

LE JARDIN
twig footstool

The painted top is a colorful contrast to the natural twig base of this stool.

COLOR PALETTE

Acrylic Craft Paints:

Baby Pink

Camel

Green Light

Heather

Lavender

Lemonade

Light Gray

Lime Yellow

Magenta

Medium Yellow

Olive Green

Pure Orange

Pure Black

Red Violet

Tangerine

Titanium White

Yellow Ochre

SURFACE
Footstool with twig base, 9" x 12", 11" tall

BRUSHES
Angulars - 1/4", 1/2"

Round - size 8

Liners - sizes 4, 6

Script Liners - sizes 2/0, 2

Scruffy brush

OTHER SUPPLIES
Matte spray sealer

PREPARE SURFACE
1. Lightly sand the top of the stool. Remove dust.
2. Apply one light coat of sealer to top. Let dry.
3. Basecoat top with Heather. Let dry.
4. Transfer the design.

continued on page 54

continued from page 52

PAINT THE DESIGN

Flowers:
1. Basecoat the rose and rosebuds with Baby Pink.
2. Float outer edges of the roses with Magenta. See the Bee & Rose Worksheet.
3. Basecoat the daffodil with Lemonade.
4. Float the outer edges of the daffodil petals with Medium Yellow.
5. Basecoat the daisy petals with Titanium White.
6. Float one side of each daisy petal with Camel.
7. Pounce the centers of the daisies with Yellow Ochre, using a scruffy brush.
8. Add a few dots to the centers of the daisies with Medium Yellow.
9. Basecoat Purple petaled flowers with Lavender.
10. Float edges of Purple petals with Red Violet.
11. Basecoat the small petaled flowers with Tangerine.
12. Float the sides of the small petals with Pure Orange.

Bee:
See the Bee and Rose Worksheet.
1. Basecoat body with Medium Yellow.
2. Basecoat wings with Titanium White.
3. Float one side of the body with Yellow Ochre.
4. Float edges of wings with Light Gray.

Leaves:
1. Basecoat leaves with Lime Yellow.
2. Float edges of large leaves with Green Light.
3. Float one side of each small leaf with Green Light.
4. Paint the outlines and linework with Olive Green.

Details:
See the Bee & Rose Worksheet.
1. Dot the centers of the small orange flowers and the daisies with Pure Black.
2. Paint the lettering and outline and add details to flowers and bee with Pure Black. Let dry completely.

FINISH

Apply two coats of spray matte sealer. Let dry between coats. ❏

BEE & ROSE WORKSHEET

Bee:

Basecoat wings with Titanium White.

Rose:
Basecoat with Baby Pink.

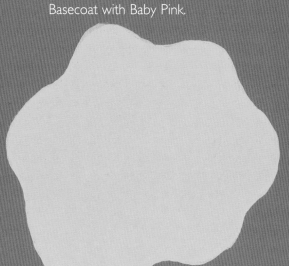

Basecoat body with Medium Yellow.

Float edges of wings with Light Gray.

Float outer edges with Magenta.

Float one side of body with Yellow Ochre.

Paint outlines and details with Pure Black.

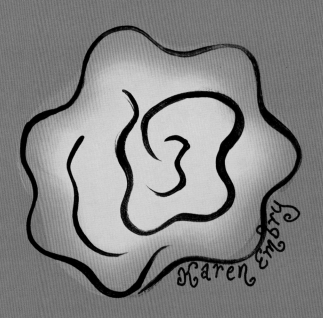

Karen Embry

55

Pattern for Footstool
(Actual Size)

Connect at dotted line to complete pattern.

SIMPLE PLEASURES
backyard swing

You can buy a wooden swing to paint or make one yourself from 3/4" or 1" thick wood.
Find a nice tree in your backyard to hang the swing from and enjoy!

COLOR PALETTE

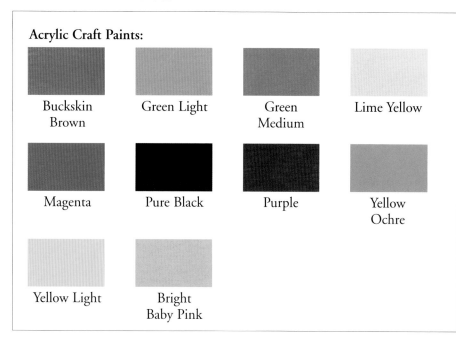

Acrylic Craft Paints:

Buckskin Brown

Green Light

Green Medium

Lime Yellow

Magenta

Pure Black

Purple

Yellow Ochre

Yellow Light

Bright Baby Pink

SURFACE
Wooden swing, 24" x 11"

BRUSHES
Angulars - 1/4", 1/2"
Rounds - size 8, 10
Script Liners - sizes 2/0, 2
Liners - sizes 2, 6
Sponge brush, 2-3" wide
Scruffy brush

OTHER SUPPLIES
Whitewash stain and sealer
If you're making your own swing, you'll need:
Nylon rope for hanging, size 3/4"
Drill and 7/8" drill bit
Outdoor sealer

PREPARE SURFACE
1. Lightly sand the wood. Wipe away all dust.
2. Apply one coat of whitewash stain and sealer. Let dry. If a stronger whitewashed look is desired, apply another coat and let dry.
3. Transfer the design.

PAINT THE DESIGN
See the Pink Flowers Worksheet.
Flowers:
1. Paint a wash of Bright Baby Pink over all petals. Let dry.
2. Paint a wash of Magenta near the centers of all the petals, walking out the color slightly towards the ends. Let dry.
3. Paint the lines in the petals with Magenta.
4. Paint stamen stems and tips with Yellow Light.
5. Paint a thin line in the center of each stamen with Yellow Ochre.
6. Using a scruffy brush, pounce Yellow Ochre at the ends of the stamen.

7. Paint a few dots at the ends of the stamen with Buckskin Brown.

Leaves & Vines:
1. Paint with a wash of Lime Yellow. Let dry.
2. Paint a wash of Green Light at the base of the leaves closest to the flowers.
3. Paint the linework on the leaves with Green Medium.

Border & Lettering:
1. Paint a wash of Purple in alternating squares around the outer edge of the swing to make a border.
2. Outline the outer border with Pure Black.
3. Paint the lettering with Pure Black. Let dry completely.

FINISH
1. Apply two coats of outdoor sealer. Let dry between coats.
2. Loop nylon rope though one hole at end of swing and back up through the other. Repeat on other side. ❏

Pink Flowers Worksheet

Fig. 1:

Wash petals with Bright Baby Pink.
Wash leaves with Lime Yellow.

Paint stamen with Yellow Light.

Pounce the tip with Yellow Ochre, using a scruffy brush.

Paint a thin line of Yellow Ochre.

Wash Magenta near center, walking out the color.

Wash Green Medium at the base of the leaves, walking out the color.

Dot stamen with Yellow Ochre.

Fig. 2:

Paint lines on petals with Magenta.

Paint linework on leaves with Green Medium.

Karen Embry

Pattern for Swing
Enlarge @250% for actual size.

TROPICAL FLAMINGOS
metal mailbox

Be sure to choose paints for this mailbox that are suitable to use on metal and for use outdoors. Follow the manufacturer's instructions for application.

COLOR PALETTE

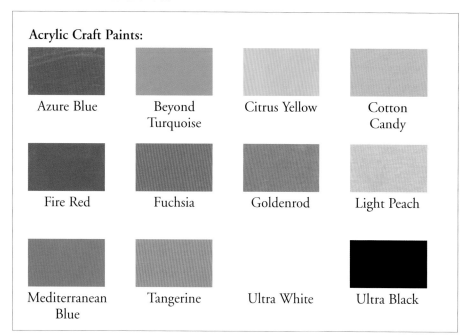

Acrylic Craft Paints:

Azure Blue   Beyond Turquoise   Citrus Yellow   Cotton Candy

Fire Red   Fuchsia   Goldenrod   Light Peach

Mediterranean Blue   Tangerine   Ultra White   Ultra Black

SURFACE
Metal mailbox

BRUSHES
Angulars - 1/4", 1/2"
Rounds - sizes 2, 4, 6
Liner - size 2

OTHER SUPPLIES
Clear gloss enamel sealer
Enamel surface conditioner

PREPARATION:
1. Wash mailbox with warm soapy water. Dry completely.
2. Apply enamel surface conditioner. Let dry.
3. Transfer pattern.

PAINT THE DESIGN
See the Flamingo Worksheet.
First Step:
1. Basecoat the flamingos' wings with Cotton Candy.
2. Basecoat flamingos' bodies with Fuchsia.
3. Basecoat the sun, the flamingos' legs, the parts of beaks near the heads, and #1 sunbeams with Citrus Yellow.
4. Basecoat the #2 sunbeams with Tangerine.
5. Basecoat the #3 sunbeams with Fire Red.
6. Basecoat the #4 sunbeams with Goldenrod.
7. Basecoat the waves with Beyond Turquoise.
8. Basecoat the water below the waves with Mediterranean Blue.
9. Basecoat the sand with Light Peach. Let dry at least one hour.

Second Step:
1. Float the bottom edge of the water with Azure Blue.
2. Float the tops of the flamingos' wings with Ultra White.
3. Paint swirls on flamingos' wings with Ultra White.
4. Paint clouds, flamingos' eyes, and dots on red sunbeams with Ultra White.
5. Paint dots in flamingos' eyes, the ends of the flamingos' beaks, the line between the wave and the water, and the line around the sun with Ultra Black. Let dry according to manufacturer's instructions.

FINISH
Apply enamel sealer. Let dry. ❏

Flamingo Worksheet

Fig. 1:
This illustration shows the basecoats and the floating on the wings.

Fig. 2:
This illustration shows the Ultra White swirl on the wings, the Ultra Black outlines, the floating on the water, and the Ultra White dots on the Fire Red sunbeams.

Karen Embry

Pattern for Mailbox
Enlarge @200% for actual size.

JUST LEAFY
planter

I painted this stylized leaf design on a simple box I built myself from 3/4" wood. You can adapt the design to fit any size planter box.

COLOR PALETTE

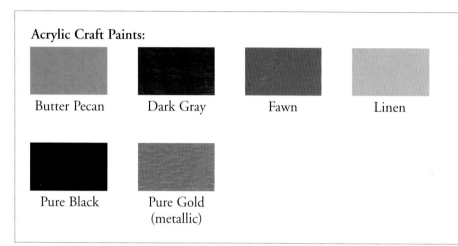

Acrylic Craft Paints:

Butter Pecan   Dark Gray   Fawn   Linen

Pure Black   Pure Gold (metallic)

SURFACE

Planter box made from 3/4" pine or cedar

4 ball knobs, 2-1/2" (for feet)

BRUSHES

Angulars - 1/2", 3/4"

Liners - sizes 2, 4

Bright - size 10

Round - size 6

OTHER SUPPLIES

Wood screws

Wood filler

Saw

Drill with screw bit

Exterior sealer

PREPARE SURFACE

1. Build the planter.
2. Fill any holes with wood filler. Let dry.
3. Sand and remove dust.
4. Seal wood. Let dry.
5. Transfer the leaf outlines. Repeat the leaf design across front and sides. Reduce to fit if needed.

BASECOAT

1. Basecoat the areas around the leaf designs on the outside of the planter with Dark Gray.
2. Basecoat the inside of the plant stand with Pure Black.
3. Basecoat all the leaves with Butter Pecan. Let dry.
4. Transfer the remainder of the designs.

PAINT THE DESIGN

See the Leaves & Swirls Worksheet.
Checked Pattern Leaves:

1. Paint the alternating leaf sections with Linen.
2. Float the edges of the Linen sections with Butter Pecan.
3. Paint the diagonal lines in the Linen areas with Butter Pecan.

Diagonal Pattern leaves:

1. Paint alternating sections of the leaves with Fawn.
2. Float the outer edges of the Butter Pecan sections of these leaves (the original basecoat) with Fawn.
3. Paint the diagonal lines in the Butter Pecan sections with Fawn.

Trim:

Paint the swirls and linework around leaves, the ball feet, and the trim with Pure Gold. Let dry completely.

FINISH

Apply two coats of exterior sealer inside and out. Let dry between coats. ❏

LEAVES & SWIRLS WORKSHEET

Dark Gray basecoat

Swirls and linework with Pure Gold

Basecoat with Butter Pecan. Float edges with Fawn.

Basecoat Butter Pecan.

Basecoat with Fawn.

Basecoat with Linen. Float edges with Butter Pecan.

Basecoat with Fawn.

Basecoat with Butter Pecan. Float edges with Fawn.

Fig. 2:

Paint lines with Fawn.

Paint lines with Butter Pecan.

Karen Embry

Pattern for Just Leafy Planter

Enlarge @ 125% for actual size.

Pattern for Girl in the Hat Stool

Enlarge @180% for actual size.
Instructions follow on page 72.

GIRL IN THE HAT

stool

A summer hat adorned with flowers was the inspiration for this stool.

COLOR PALETTE

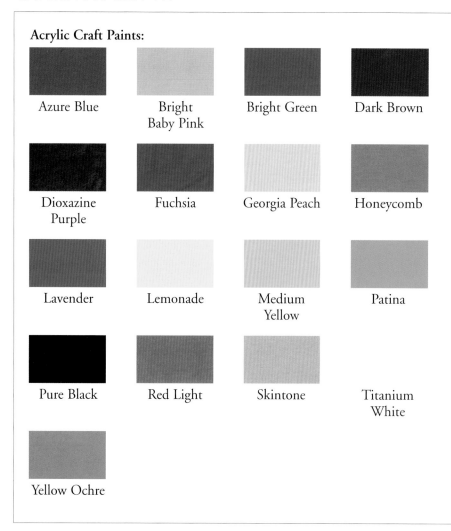

Acrylic Craft Paints:

Azure Blue

Bright Baby Pink

Bright Green

Dark Brown

Dioxazine Purple

Fuchsia

Georgia Peach

Honeycomb

Lavender

Lemonade

Medium Yellow

Patina

Pure Black

Red Light

Skintone

Titanium White

Yellow Ochre

SURFACE

Wooden bar stool, 30" tall

BRUSHES

Liners - sizes 2, 4

Rounds - sizes 2, 4, 6

Brights - sizes 8, 10

Script - size 4

Square Wash - 1"

OTHER SUPPLIES

Brush-on varnish, satin sheen

Blending gel medium

PREPARE SURFACE

1. Sand stool. Wipe away dust.
2. Apply sealer. Let dry.
3. Transfer the design.

PAINT THE LEGS

1. Basecoat one leg with Bright Green, one with Purple, one with Fuchsia, and one with Azure Blue.
2. Paint the stretchers with Titanium White.
3. Paint swirls on the stretchers with Pure Black.

PAINT THE TOP

Face:

1. Basecoat skin with Georgia Peach.
2. Float sides of face, around nose, and under chin with Skintone.
3. Paint lips with Red Light.
4. Dry brush highlights on lips with Bright Baby Pink.
5. Paint irises of eyes with Dark Brown.
6. Paint pupils with Pure Black.
7. Paint the sclera (whites of the eyes) with Titanium White.
8. Mix equal amounts Dark Brown and Honeycomb. Paint eyelashes and eyebrows.

Hair:

1. Basecoat hair with Dark Brown.
2. Brush in Honeycomb highlights.

Dress:

1. Basecoat with Purple.
2. While basecoat is still wet, brush blending gel medium on dress and slip-slap Lavender on top edge.

Background:

1. Basecoat the grassy area with Bright Green.
2. While basecoat is still wet, brush grass with blending gel medium and slip-slap with Medium Yellow.
3. Basecoat the sky with Azure Blue.
4. Brush blending gel medium on the sky. Slip-slap with Patina and blend.

continued on page 75

Summer Roses Worksheet

Fig. 1:

Basecoat with Dioxazine Purple.

Brush blending gel medium over rose, then apply Lavender in a choppy circular pattern.

Basecoat with Medium Yellow. Brush blending gel medium over rose, then apply Lemonade in a choppy circular pattern.

Basecoat leaf with Bright Green. Apply blending gel medium to leaf. Blend Medium Yellow on the tip.

Fig. 2:

While still wet, apply Titanium White in a choppy circular pattern to both roses.

While leaf is still wet, apply Green Forest to base of leaf and blend.

continued from page 72

Hat:
1. Basecoat with Fuchsia.
2. Brush with blending gel medium. Slip-slap Bright Baby Pink + a touch of Titanium White on the top of the brim.
3. Slip-slap a touch of Purple + blending gel medium on the underside near the hair.

Roses & Hat Band:
1. Basecoat the front rose and the hat band with Dioxazine Purple.
2. Brush blending gel medium on rose. Brush Lavender in a choppy circular pattern. See the Summer Roses Worksheet, Fig. 1.
3. While blending gel medium is still wet, brush on Titanium White in a choppy circular pattern. See the Summer Roses Worksheet, Fig. 2.
4. Basecoat the back rose with Medium Yellow. See the Summer Roses Worksheet, Fig. 1.
5. Brush blending gel medium on rose and brush on Lemonade in a choppy circular pattern.
6. While still wet, brush on Titanium White in a choppy circular pattern. See the Summer Roses Worksheet, Fig. 2.
7. Basecoat leaves with Bright Green.
8. Brush blending gel medium on each leaf.
9. Blend a touch of Medium Yellow at the tip. See the worksheet, Fig. 1.
10. Blend a touch of Green Forest at the base of each leaf. See the worksheet, Fig. 2.

Edge:
Paint the checks with Titanium White and Pure Black. Let dry completely.

FINISH
Brush with two coats satin varnish. Let dry between coats. ❏

GREETING ANGEL
garden ornament & planter box

Let this smiling angel welcome guests to your garden. You can build her yourself,
using the patterns provided.

COLOR PALETTE

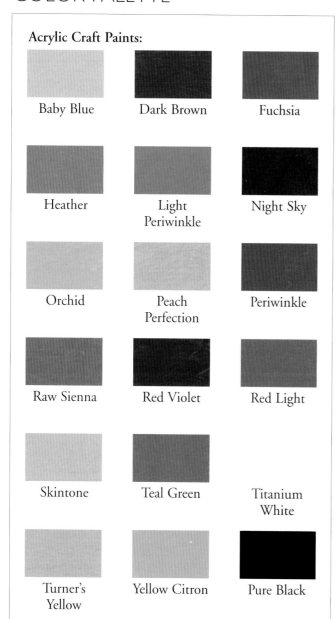

Acrylic Craft Paints:

Baby Blue | Dark Brown | Fuchsia

Heather | Light Periwinkle | Night Sky

Orchid | Peach Perfection | Periwinkle

Raw Sienna | Red Violet | Red Light

Skintone | Teal Green | Titanium White

Turner's Yellow | Yellow Citron | Pure Black

SURFACE
Angel cut from 1/2" or 3/4" exterior plywood, using the pattern provided

BRUSHES
Angulars - 1/4", 1/2", 3/4"
Liners - sizes 2, 4, 6
Bright - size 10
Rounds - sizes 2, 4, 6, 8, 10
Square Wash - 1"
Script Liners - sizes 2/0, 0, 2, 4

OTHER SUPPLIES
9 drywall screws, 1-1/4"
2 wooden stakes, each 2" wide, 3 ft. long
Jigsaw
Outdoor sealer with UV protection, matte or satin sheen

PREPARE SURFACE
1. Cut out angel.
2. Sand pieces. Wipe away dust.
3. Seal the wood.
4. Transfer the design.

PAINT THE ANGEL
See the Hand & Rose Worksheet.
Face:
1. Basecoat face with Skintone.
2. Float around face, under chin, above neckline, and on the left side of the nose with Peach Perfection.
3. Paint lips with Red Light.
4. Paint teeth with Titanium White.
5. Mix equal amounts Turner's Yellow and Raw Sienna. Paint eyebrows.
6. Paint eyelashes with Dark Brown.

continued on page 79

HAND & ROSE WORKSHEET

Fig. 1:
Paint rose with Orchid.
Paint leaves with Yellow Citron.
Float bottom edge of rose with Fuchsia.
Paint fingers with Skintone.
Paint nails with Red Light.

Fig. 2:
Paint swirls with Pure Black.
Float sides of fingers with Peach Perfection

Karen Embry

continued from page 76

Hair:
1. Basecoat with Turner's Yellow.
2. Float around the outer edges with Raw Sienna.
3. Add lines with Raw Sienna.

Wings:
1. Basecoat inner area with Orchid.
2. Float around all edges with Fuchsia.
3. Basecoat the outer areas with Light Periwinkle.
4. Float edges with Periwinkle.
5. Paint swirls with Periwinkle.

Heart & Borders:
1. Paint center of heart with Red Light.
2. Paint dots in center of heart with Titanium White.
3. Paint checks around edges of heart, at waist, below first band on skirt, and at bottom of skirt with Pure Black and Titanium White.

First Section of Skirt:
1. Basecoat with Yellow Citron.
2. Float top and bottom edges with Teal Green.
3. Paint the arch design with Teal Green.

Second Section of Skirt:
1. Basecoat with Heather.
2. Float top and bottom edges with Red Violet.
3. Paint roses with Orchid.
4. Float bottom edges of roses with Fuchsia.
5. Paint leaves with Yellow Citron.
6. Paint dots with Titanium White.
7. Paint swirls in rosebuds with Pure Black.

Third & Fifth Sections of Skirt:
1. Basecoat with Baby Blue.
2. Float top and bottom edges with Light Periwinkle.
3. Paint vertical lines with Light Periwinkle.

Fourth Section of Skirt:
1. Basecoat with Teal Green.
2. Paint leaves with Yellow Citron.
3. Paint trim at edges with Turner's Yellow.

Bottom Section of Skirt:
1. Paint with Orchid.
2. Float upper edge with Fuchsia.
3. Paint dots with Fuchsia.

PAINT THE PLANTER BOX

Basecoats:
1. Basecoat inside box with Orchid.
2. Basecoat front with Heather.
3. Basecoat sides of box with Baby Blue.
4. Transfer the pattern.

Sides:
1. Float the sides with Light Periwinkle.
2. Paint the vertical stripes on the sides with Light Periwinkle.

Front:
1. Paint the hands with Skintone.
2. Float the sides of the hands and fingers with Peach Perfection.
3. Paint nails with Red Light.
4. Paint roses with Orchid. Float bottoms with Fuchsia.
5. Paint leaves with Yellow Citron.
6. Paint happy face with Turner's Yellow. Float bottom with Raw Sienna.
7. Paint the circle around the peace sign with Baby Blue.
8. Paint heart with Red Light.
9. Paint checks around edges of heart and on top and sides with Pure Black and Titanium White.
10. Paint lettering, swirls in roses, outline of the peace sign, and happy face eyes and mouth with Pure Black.
11. Paint dots on front with Titanium White. Let dry completely.

FINISH
1. Apply two coats of outdoor matte or satin sealer.
2. Attach two stakes to the back of the angel with screws.
3. Attach the planter box to the front of the angel by securing from the back with screws. See the pattern for screw placement. ❑

Patterns for Garden Ornament & Planter Box
Enlarge @ 250 % for actual size.

TOP SECTION

Reverse and repeat
wing section on opposite
side.

Enlarge @ 250% for actual size.

Front of Planter Box
Enlarge @ 200% for actual size.

Patterns for Garden Ornament & Planter Box

Enlarge @ 250% for actual size.

CENTER SECTION

Placement holes for screws

Bottom edge of plant box rests on this line

BOTTOM SECTION

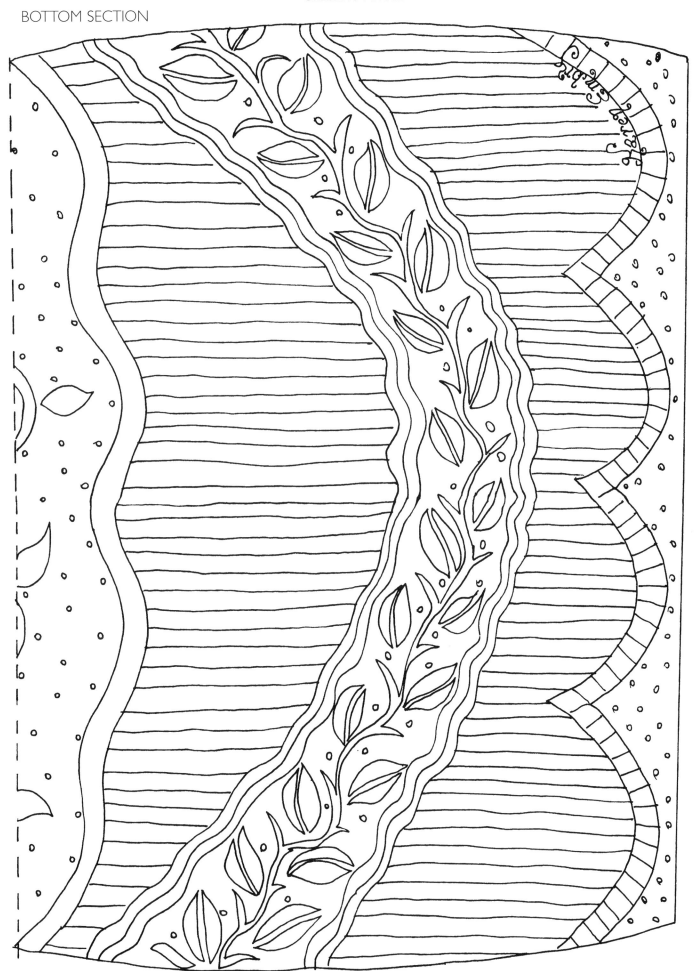

MAKE A WISH
trinket boxes

These little papier mache boxes are easy to paint. The knobs on their tops are drawer pulls purchased at my local home and garden center. No prep work is necessary for papier mache. When you've finished painting, fill them with trinkets and wishes.

COLOR PALETTE

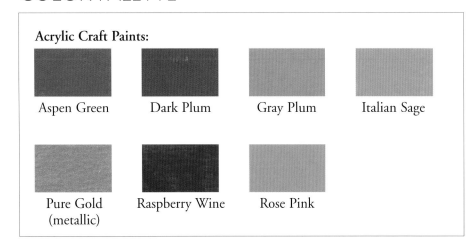

Acrylic Craft Paints:

Aspen Green	Dark Plum	Gray Plum	Italian Sage
Pure Gold (metallic)	Raspberry Wine	Rose Pink	

SURFACES
3 papier mache boxes, 2-1/2" diameter

BRUSHES
Angulars - 1/4", 1/2"
Bright - size 10
Round - size 2
Liner - size 2

OTHER SUPPLIES
3 drawer pulls
Sealer spray - satin

PAINT THE DESIGNS

See the Make a Wish Worksheet.

Pink Box:

1. Basecoat the bottom with Rose Pink.
2. Basecoat the lid with Raspberry Wine.
3. Float the edges of the bottom with Raspberry Wine.
4. Paint the lettering and trim with Pure Gold.

Green Box:

1. Basecoat the bottom with Italian Sage.
2. Basecoat the lid with Aspen Green.
3. Float the edges of the bottom with Aspen Green.

4. Paint the lettering and trim with Pure Gold .

Purple Box:

1. Basecoat the bottom with Gray Plum.
2. Basecoat the lid with Dark Plum.
3. Float the edges of the bottom with Dark Plum.
4. Paint the lettering and trim with Pure Gold. Let dry completely.

FINISH

1. Apply one coat of satin sealer. Let dry.
2. Attach knobs to tops of boxes. ❏

Patterns for Trinket Boxes

Enlarge @155% for actual size.

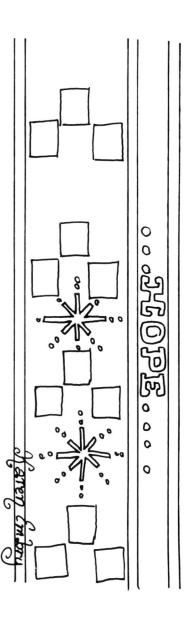

Make a Wish Worksheet

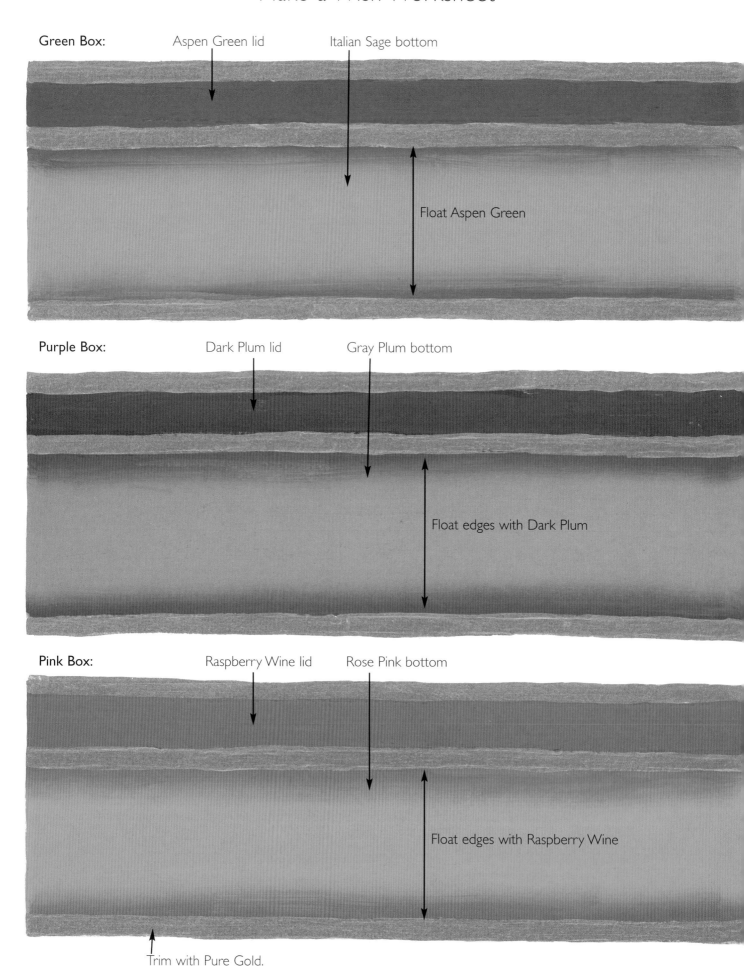

Green Box: Aspen Green lid   Italian Sage bottom

Float Aspen Green

Purple Box: Dark Plum lid   Gray Plum bottom

Float edges with Dark Plum

Pink Box: Raspberry Wine lid   Rose Pink bottom

Float edges with Raspberry Wine

Trim with Pure Gold.

Add lettering and designs with Pure Gold.

ONCE UPON A TIME
toy chest

I combined familiar images from several fairy tales to create the scene I painted on this toy chest – there's Little Red Riding Hood with her basket, Cinderella's pumpkin coach, the three little pigs, and the frog prince. The lid is hinged for storage.

COLOR PALETTE

Acrylic Craft Paints:

Apple Spice	Bayberry	Blue Ribbon	Bright Baby Pink
Burnt Umber	Butter Pecan	Country Twill	Dark Brown
French Blue	Fresh Foliage	Georgia Peach	Green Umber
Hot Pink	Inca Gold (metallic)	Light Blue	Light Gray
Medium Gray	Mint Green	Pure Black	Red Light
Tangerine	Teddy Bear Brown	Terra Cotta	Wicker White
Yellow Light	Yellow Ochre		

SURFACE
Wooden storage bench/toy chest

BRUSHES
Scruffy Brushes - sizes 2, 4, 6, 8

Brights - sizes 6, 10

Liners - sizes 2, 4

Round - sizes 2, 6, 10

Script Liner - sizes 2/0, 2, 4

Angulars - 1/8", 1/4", 1/2", 3/4"

Square Wash - 1"

OTHER SUPPLIES
Blending gel medium

Alphabet stencil

Stencil brush

Brush-on satin varnish

PREPARE SURFACE
1. Sand chest. Wipe away dust.
2. Brush on wood sealer. Let dry.
3. Transfer pattern outlines for sky and grass.
4. Basecoat grass with Fresh Foliage. Float with Green Umber.
5. Basecoat sky with French Blue.
6. Mix equal amounts of French Blue and Wicker White. Use this mixture to brush the clouds.
7. Basecoat top of chest with Butter Pecan. Let dry.
8. Transfer the remainder of the pattern.

PAINT THE DESIGN
Frog:

See the Frog Worksheet.
1. Paint the frog with Bayberry.
2. Float the top of the frog's back, the top of his nose, and his legs with Wicker White.
3. Float the bottom with Burnt Umber.
4. Mix three parts blending gel medium with seven parts Burnt Umber and paint the frog's spots. (The blending gel makes the paint somewhat transparent.)
5. Paint the eye with Yellow Ochre.
6. Paint the iris with Pure Black. Highlight with Wicker White.
7. Paint crown with Inca Gold.
8. Float bottom of crown with Burnt Umber and paint the line at the bottom edge with Burnt Umber.
9. Paint the jewels on the crown with Red Light and Blue Ribbon.

Pumpkin Coach:
1. Basecoat the pumpkin with Tangerine.
2. Float pumpkin sections with Terra Cotta.
3. Basecoat the door with Terra Cotta.
4. Float edges of the door with Burnt Umber.
5. Outline the door with Inca Gold.
6. Paint leaves on top with Fresh Foliage.
7. Float tops of leaves with Wicker White.
8. Float bottoms of leaves with Green Umber. Paint veins with Green Umber.
9. Paint stem with Dark Brown.
10. Paint swirling vines with Inca Gold and Green Umber.
11. Paint wheels with Wicker White.
12. Paint shadows on wheels with medium gray.

Trees:
1. Paint trunks with Dark Brown.
2. Highlight trunks with Country Twill.
3. Paint first layer of leaves with Green Umber, second layer with Fresh Foliage, and third layer with mint green.
4. Paint veins in leaves with Burnt Umber.

Mice:
1. Paint mice with Light Gray.
2. Float tops with Wicker White.
3. Float bottoms with medium gray.
4. Paint inside ears with Baby Pink.
5. Float inside ears with Hot Pink.
6. Paint noses with Bright Baby Pink.
7. Highlight noses with Wicker White.
8. Paint eyes with Pure Black.
9. Paint whiskers with Burnt Umber.

Pigs:
1. Paint with Bright Baby Pink.
2. Float bottom sides with Hot Pink.
3. Float tops with Wicker White.
4. Paint ears and noses with Hot Pink.
5. Float ears with Bright Baby Pink. Paint nostrils in snouts with Bright Baby Pink.
6. Paint eyes with Pure Black.
7. Paint tiny Wicker White highlights in each eye.

Path:
1. Paint with Light Gray.
2. Paint stones with Country Twill.
3. Float stones with Burnt Umber.
4. Dry brush stones with Wicker White.

Shrubs:
1. Using a scruffy brush, pounce background of shrubs next to the path with Burnt Umber.
2. Pounce next layer with Fresh Foliage, letting some Burnt Umber show through.
3. Pounce the third layer with Bayberry, letting some of the previous colors show through.

Flowers:
1. Paint lower petals of pink flowers with Hot Pink. Paint upper petals with Bright Baby Pink.

continued on page 92

Frog Worksheet

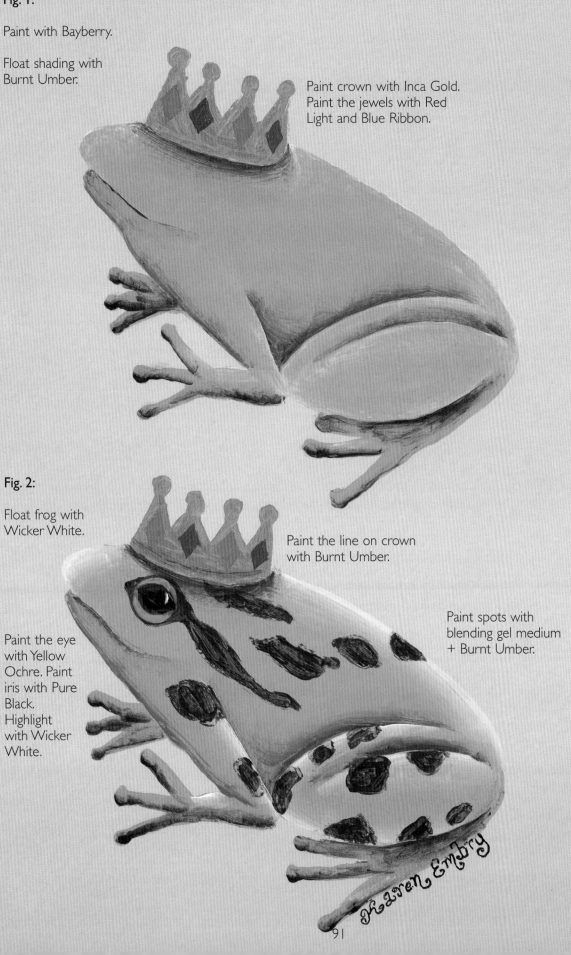

Fig. 1:

Paint with Bayberry.

Float shading with Burnt Umber.

Paint crown with Inca Gold. Paint the jewels with Red Light and Blue Ribbon.

Fig. 2:

Float frog with Wicker White.

Paint the line on crown with Burnt Umber.

Paint the eye with Yellow Ochre. Paint iris with Pure Black. Highlight with Wicker White.

Paint spots with blending gel medium + Burnt Umber.

Karen Embry

continued from page 90

2. Paint lower petals of blue flowers with Blue Ribbon. Paint upper petals with Light Blue.
3. Paint centers with Yellow Light. Dot with Yellow Ochre.
4. Paint groups of three dots around the flowers with Wicker White.

Girl:
1. Paint cape with Red Light.
2. Float cape with Apple Spice.
3. Paint face, legs, and hands with Georgia Peach.
4. Paint shoes with Pure Black.
5. Paint dress with Bright Baby Pink.
6. Paint stripes on dress with Wicker White.
7. Paint lips with Bright Baby Pink.
8. Paint bangs, eyebrows, nose, and eyes with Teddy Bear Brown.
9. Paint pupils with Pure Black.
10. Paint trim on cape with Inca Gold.

Basket:
1. Paint basket with Teddy Bear Brown.
2. Float bottom with Dark Brown.
3. Float of top with Wicker White.
4. Paint basketweave with Burnt Umber.

STENCIL

Stencil "Once Upon a Time" with Pure Black, using alphabet stencil. Let dry completely.

FINISH

Brush on two coats of satin varnish. Let dry between coats. ❏

Patterns for Toy Chest
Enlarge @175% for actual size.

92

Connect pattern at dotted lines to complete.

BLOOMING IVY
adirondack chair & table

This table and chair become a pair when they are painted with coordinating motifs. Using a coordinated design is an easy way to create a unified look from separate pieces.

COLOR PALETTE

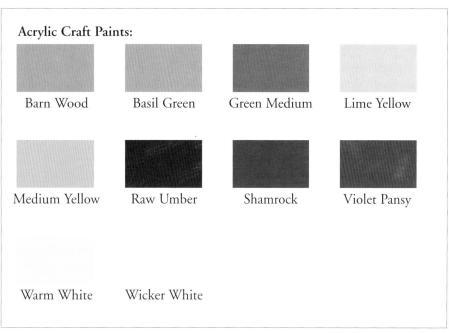

Acrylic Craft Paints:

Barn Wood	Basil Green	Green Medium	Lime Yellow
Medium Yellow	Raw Umber	Shamrock	Violet Pansy
Warm White	Wicker White		

SURFACES
Wooden Adirondack chair
Small wooden table

BRUSHES
Rounds - sizes 4, 6
Liner - size 2
Script Liner - size 2
Angular - 1/4"
Sponge brush

OTHER SUPPLIES
Primer
Foam roller, 3" or 4"
Exterior waterbase varnish, satin

PREPARE SURFACE
1. Sand the chair and table. Remove dust with a tack cloth.
2. Apply primer to knotholes. Let dry.
3. Apply a coat of sealer. Let dry.
4. Base paint the chair and table with Lime Yellow. Let dry.
5. Transfer the pattern.

continued on page 96

Continued from page 95

PAINT THE DESIGN

See the Ivy Vine Worksheet.

Ivy:

1. Basecoat the leaves on the table and chair with Basil Green.
2. Paint the vines and the veins with Green Medium.
3. Paint the shadow behind each leaf with a mix of equal amounts of Green Medium and Raw Umber.
4. Float the shadow side of each leaf with Warm White.
5. Float the other half of each leaf including the area near the center vein with Green Medium.

Flowers:

1. Paint the flower petals with Violet Pansy.
2. Paint the center of each flower with Medium Yellow.

Dragonfly:

1. Basecoat the dragonfly wings with Wicker White.
2. Basecoat the dragonfly body with Shamrock.
3. Paint the shadows of the body and wings with Barn Wood.
4. Paint the lines in the wings with Barn Wood. Let dry completely.

FINISH

Brush on two coats of exterior varnish. Let dry between coats. ❏

Ivy Vine Worksheet

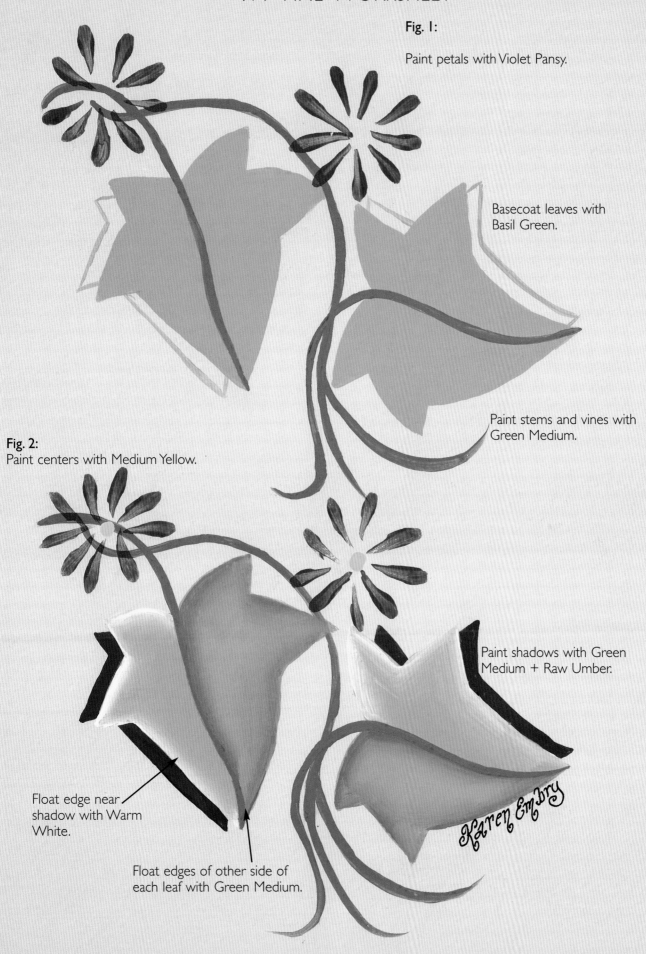

Fig. 1:

Paint petals with Violet Pansy.

Basecoat leaves with Basil Green.

Paint stems and vines with Green Medium.

Fig. 2:
Paint centers with Medium Yellow.

Paint shadows with Green Medium + Raw Umber.

Float edge near shadow with Warm White.

Float edges of other side of each leaf with Green Medium.

Karen Embry

Pattern for Blooming Ivy Adirondack Chair & Table
(Actual size)

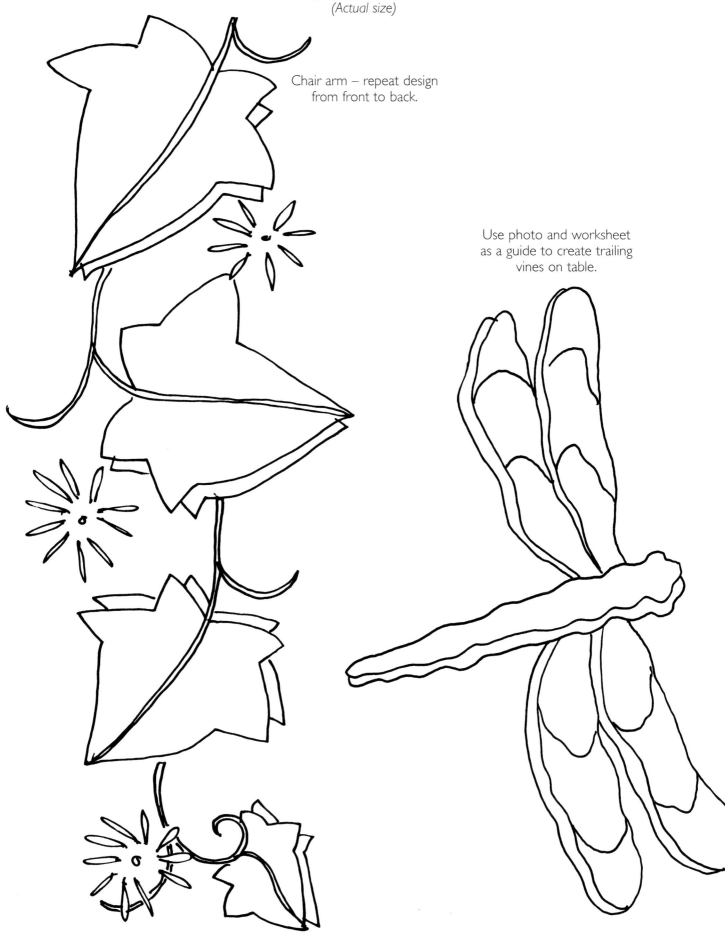

Chair arm – repeat design
from front to back.

Use photo and worksheet
as a guide to create trailing
vines on table.

Pattern for Just for Her Cabinet

Additional patterns for this project appear on page 104
Enlarge @ 145% for actual size.

Just for You

Continue ribbon
down size of cabinet.

JUST FOR HER
cabinet

This cabinet started out as an unfinished bedside table. It's a fun piece for
a bathroom or dressing room.

COLOR PALETTE

Acrylic Craft Paints:

Azure Blue   Bright Green   Country Twill   Engine Red

Green Forest   Hot Pink   Inca Gold (metallic)   Italian Sage

Lavender   Light Gray   Magenta   Maple Syrup

Pink   Pure Black   Purple   Raw Umber

Tapioca   Wicker White   Yellow Light   Yellow Ochre

SURFACE
Wooden cabinet

BRUSHES
Angulars - 1/4", 1/2"

Script Liner - sizes 2/0, 2

Liners - sizes 2, 4

Rounds - sizes 2, 4, 6

Brights - sizes 6, 8, 10

OTHER SUPPLIES
Blending gel medium

Satin varnish

PREPARE SURFACE
1. Sand cabinet. Wipe away dust.
2. Brush on wood sealer. Let dry.
3. Transfer the outline of the dresser scarf.

4. Base paint the dresser scarf with Tapioca.
5. Base paint the rest of the cabinet with Italian Sage.
6. Transfer the rest of the design.

PAINT THE DESIGN
Ribbon:
1. Basecoat with Azure Blue.
2. Float edges with Wicker White.

Mirror:
1. Basecoat the frame with Purple.
2. Apply a light coat of blending gel medium to the frame. Lightly blend some Lavender over the frame. Let dry.
3. Paint the trim on the frame with Inca Gold.
4. On the gold trim, paint a few Yellow Light highlights.
5. Basecoat the mirror with Wicker White.
6. Apply a thin coat of blending gel medium to the mirror, then lightly blend in some Light Gray in a diagonal manner.

Pearls:
1. Basecoat with Wicker White.
2. Float edges with Light Gray.

Keys:
1. Basecoat with Wicker White.
2. Float edges with Light Gray.
3. Basecoat the ribbon with Hot Pink.
4. Highlight the ribbon with pink.

Card:
See the Just for You Worksheet.
1. Basecoat with Wicker White.
2. Float edges with Light Gray.
3. Paint the hole with Light Gray.
4. Paint the string with Raw Umber.
5. Highlight the string with Tapioca.

continued on page 102

continued from page 100

6. Paint the words "Just for You" with Raw Umber. Paint the squiggles with Raw Umber.

Nail Polish Bottles:

1. Basecoat tops with Pure Black.
2. Float sides of tops with Light Gray.
3. Paint a white highlight on each top.
4. Basecoat the front bottle with Engine Red.
5. Basecoat the back bottle with Hot Pink.
6. Float the tops of both bottles with Wicker White.

Watch:

1. Basecoat the band and case with Country Twill.
2. Float edges with Maple Syrup.
3. Paint watch face with Wicker White. Paint a few Wicker White highlights on the band.
4. Paint the lines on the face and the hands with Maple Syrup.

Charm Bracelet:

1. Mix equal amounts Yellow Ochre and Maple Syrup. Basecoat chain.
2. Basecoat the charms with Yellow Ochre.
3. Float one side of each charm with Maple Syrup.
4. Brush Wicker White highlights on the other sides of the charms.

Roses:

See the Just for You Worksheet. All the roses are painted the same way.

1. Basecoat flowers with Hot Pink.
2. Brush blending gel on flowers and brush Magenta near bases of petals.
3. Brush on a thin coat of blending gel and blend Wicker White at the tips of the petals.
4. Basecoat the leaves and stems with Bright Green.
5. Brush blending gel medium on the leaves and stems. Stroke Green Forest at the bases of the leaves and along the stems. Blend.

Dresser Scarf:

See the Just for You Worksheet.

1. Float around the outside edges of all the items on the dresser scarf with Raw Umber.
2. Paint the tiny holes around the edges with Raw Umber. Let dry completely.

FINISH

Brush on two coats of satin varnish. Let dry between coats. ❏

JUST FOR YOU WORKSHEET

Fig. 1:

Basecoat with Hot Pink.
Brush with blending gel medium and
blend Magenta near bases of petals.

Basecoat with
Tapioca.

Basecoat with Wicker
White.
Float inside edges
with Light Gray.

Float around card
and roses with
Raw Umber.

Blend Wicker White in
center of rose petals.

Fig. 2:

Float with Raw Umber.

Highlight
with Tapioca.

Paint with
Raw Umber.

Just for You

Karen Embry

Brush blending gel medium on leaves
and stems. Blend Green Forest near
bases of leaves and along stems.

103

Patterns for Just for Her Cabinet

Additional patterns appear on page 99.
Enlarge @ 130% for actual size.

Use photo as a guide
to create trailing roses
on sides of cabinet.

Pattern for Summertime Coverup Fireplace Screen

Additional patterns appear on page 109.
Enlarge @ 230% for actual size.

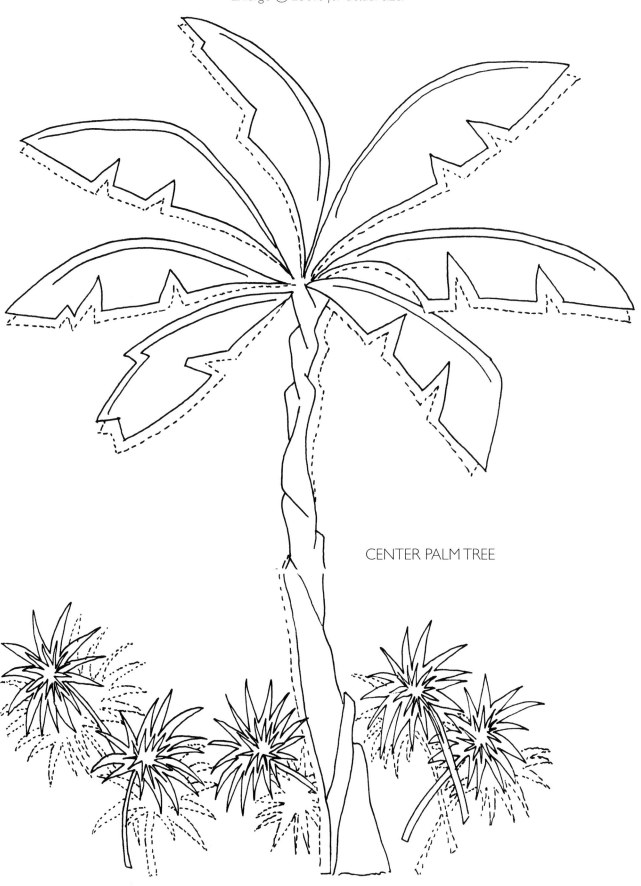

CENTER PALM TREE

SUMMERTIME COVERUP
fireplace screen

A painted screen makes a fireplace a focal point even in the summer.

COLOR PALETTE

Acrylic Craft Paints:

Apple Spice	Burnt Carmine	Burnt Umber	Camel
Coffee Bean	Country Twill	Gray Green	Green Medium
Italian Sage	Olive Green	Pure Gold (metallic)	Raw Sienna
Tapioca			

SURFACE
Wooden fireplace screen

BRUSHES
Angulars - 1/4", 1/2", 3/4"

Rounds - sizes 2, 4, 6

Brights - sizes 6, 8

Liner - sizes 2, 4

Script Liner - size 2

OTHER SUPPLIES
Matte spray sealer

PREPARE SURFACE
1. Sand screen. Wipe away dust.
2. Seal wood with wood sealer. Let dry.
3. Base paint with two coats Tapioca. Let dry between coats.
4. Transfer pattern.

continued on page 109

Palm & Print Worksheet

SMALL PALM TREES

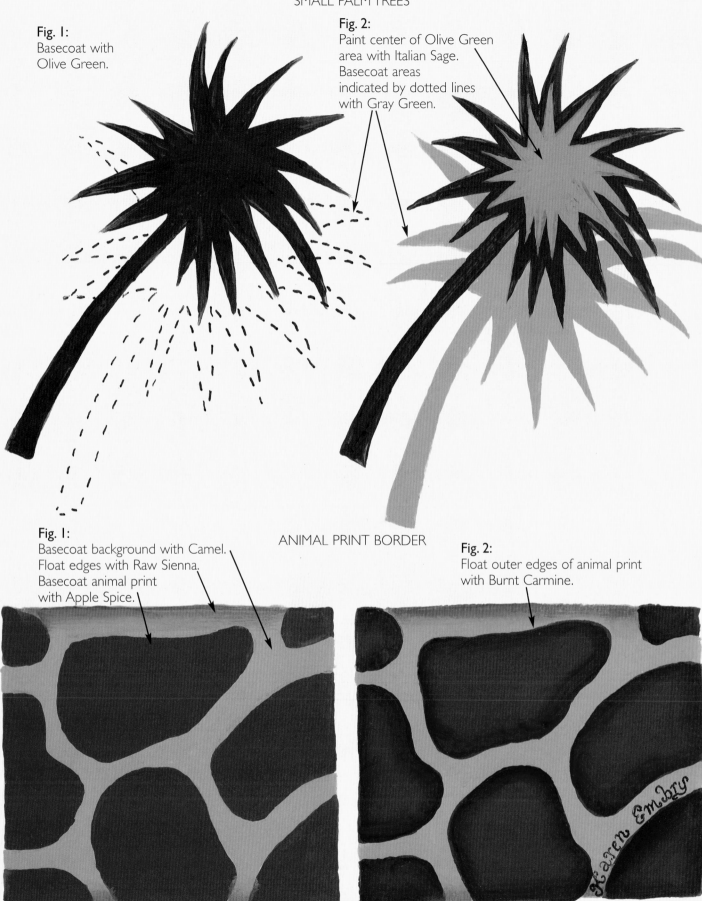

Fig. 1:
Basecoat with
Olive Green.

Fig. 2:
Paint center of Olive Green
area with Italian Sage.
Basecoat areas
indicated by dotted lines
with Gray Green.

ANIMAL PRINT BORDER

Fig. 1:
Basecoat background with Camel.
Float edges with Raw Sienna.
Basecoat animal print
with Apple Spice.

Fig. 2:
Float outer edges of animal print
with Burnt Carmine.

Karen Embry

continued from page 106

PAINT THE DESIGN

Animal Print Border:

See the Palm & Print Worksheet.

1. Basecoat with Camel.
2. Float edges with Raw Sienna.
3. Paint the areas that resemble animal spots with Apple Spice.
4. Float the edges of these areas with Burnt Carmine.
5. Paint the 3/4" band inside the border with Pure Gold.
6. Float inside the band with Camel.

Large Palm Trees:

1. Basecoat the trunks with Country Twill.
2. Float edges with Coffee Bean.
3. Basecoat fronds with Green Medium.
4. Float bottoms of fronds with Olive Green.
5. Paint a line across the top of each frond with Italian Sage.

Small Palm Trees:

See the Palm & Print Worksheet.

1. Basecoat the shadows (indicated on the pattern by dotted lines) with Gray Green.
2. Basecoat the small trees with Olive Green.
3. Paint the inner area of the fronds with Italian Sage. Let dry completely.

FINISH

Apply two coats of satin sealer. Let dry in between coats. ❑

Border – Enlarge @ 120% for actual size.

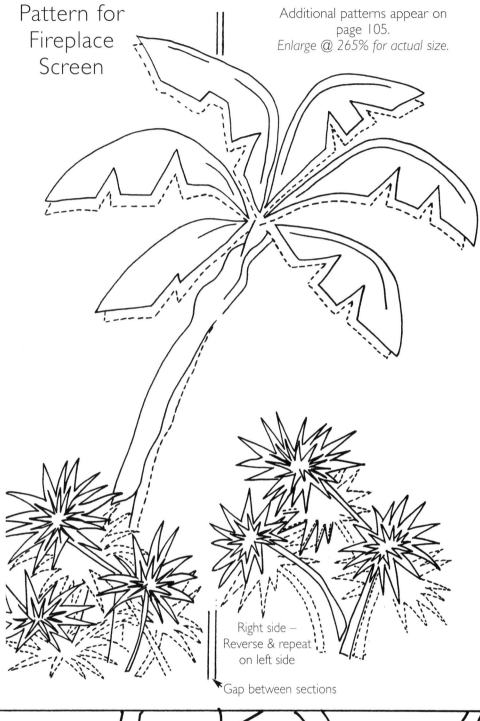

Pattern for Fireplace Screen

Additional patterns appear on page 105.
Enlarge @ 265% for actual size.

Right side –
Reverse & repeat on left side

Gap between sections

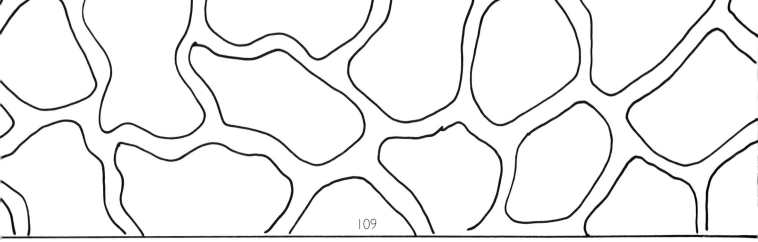

BELIEVE IN YOURSELF
Painted Pillow

Paint this pillow for yourself as a gentle reminder or as a present for a friend whose self-confidence needs a boost.

COLOR PALETTE

Acrylic Craft Paints:

 Baby Pink

 Baby Blue

 Fresh Foliage

Hot Pink

 Lime Light

 Night Sky

 Pure Black

 Red Light

Titanium White

SURFACE

Canvas pillow cover with flange, 17" x 18"

Pillow insert, 14"

BRUSHES

Round - size 4

Angulars - 1/4", 1/2"

Liner - size 2

Script Liner - size 2/0

OTHER SUPPLIES

Textile medium

Cardboard or poster board cut to fit inside pillow cover

Plastic sheeting

Tape

PREPARE SURFACE

1. Wrap cardboard or poster board with plastic. Tape in place. Insert in pillow. (This protects the back side of the pillow cover from paint seeping through.)
2. Transfer the design.
3. Mix paint and textile medium according to manufacturer's instructions. *Tips:* I use textile medium instead of water to thin paint when painting on fabric. I also recommend textile medium as a blending or floating agent when painting on fabric.

continued on page 113

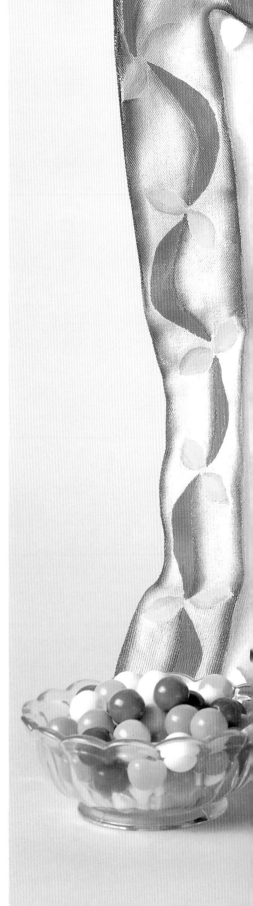

Pillow Worksheet

Fig. 1:

Basecoat with Baby Blue.

Paint ribbon with Red Light.

Paint leaves with Lime Light.

Basecoat with Baby Pink.

Paint dots and letters with Titanium White.

Fig. 2:

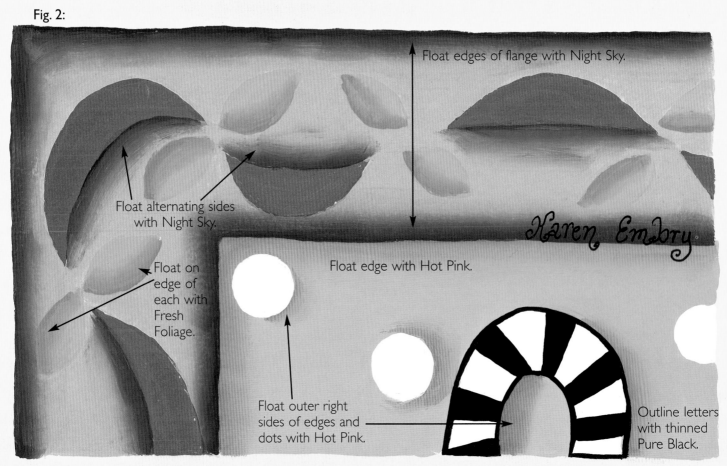

Float edges of flange with Night Sky.

Float alternating sides with Night Sky.

Float on edge of each with Fresh Foliage.

Float edge with Hot Pink.

Karen Embry

Float outer right sides of edges and dots with Hot Pink.

Outline letters with thinned Pure Black.

continued from page 110

PAINT THE DESIGN

See the Pillow Worksheet.

Center Design:

1. Basecoat the center square of the pillow Baby Pink.
2. Paint the dots with Titanium White.
3. Paint the letters with Titanium White.
4. Paint the stripes on the letters with Pure Black.
5. Outline the letters with Pure Black that has been thinned with textile medium.

Border:

1. Paint the leaves on the flange with Lime Light.
2. Paint the ribbon with Red Light.
3. Paint the rest of the flange with Baby Blue.

Shading:

1. Float the outer edge of the center square with Hot Pink.
2. On the outer right sides of the letters and the dots, float Hot Pink.
3. Float the inner and outer edges of the flange with Night Sky.
4. Float alternating sides on the outside of the ribbon with Night Sky.
5. Float the edge of one side of each leaf with Fresh Foliage. Let dry completely.

FINISH

1. Heat set the painted design according to the textile medium manufacturer's instructions.
2. Place pillow insert in pillow. ❑

Pattern for Pillow Cover

Enlarge @ 200% for actual size.

Continue border around all four sides.

HYDRANGEA WELCOME
salvaged window

I found this old window at a flea market. I added heart-shaped wooden cutouts for dimensional leaves and wooden numbers for the street address to make it a great wall decoration. I used acrylic craft paints on the wood frame, cutouts, and letters and weatherproof enamels to paint on the glass.

COLOR PALETTE

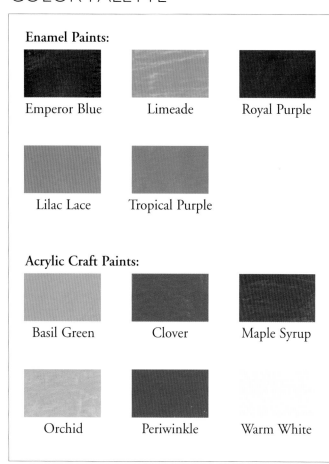

Enamel Paints:

Emperor Blue | Limeade | Royal Purple

Lilac Lace | Tropical Purple

Acrylic Craft Paints:

Basil Green | Clover | Maple Syrup

Orchid | Periwinkle | Warm White

SURFACE
Window sash with glass, 3 ft. wide, 2 ft. tall

BRUSHES
Filbert - size 8   Round - size 2

Square Wash - 1"   Script Liner - size 2

1" foam brush

OTHER SUPPLIES
Crackle medium

Exterior waterbase varnish, satin

9 extra large primitive wood hearts

2 heavy screw eyes, 1"

6 ft. white chain

Wooden numbers, 5" tall (for your address)

White transfer paper

Clear gloss enamel sealer

Enamel surface conditioner

Waterproof glue

PREPARE SURFACE
1. Wash window frame with warm soapy water.
2. Remove all dirt and any greasy residue from glass.
3. Brush enamel surface conditioner on the glass. Let dry.

PAINT THE DESIGN
Flowers:
See the Hydrangea Worksheet.
1. Slip-slap Emperor Blue + Royal Purple on the background area of the flowers. Let dry.
2. Lightly transfer the petal pattern.
3. Mix equal amounts of Emperor Blue and Purple. Double load one side of the filbert brush with this mix and the other side with Tropical Purple. Paint the petals in the first bunch of flowers.
4. Double load the filbert brush with Lilac Lace and Tropical Purple. Paint the petals in the second bunch of flowers. Alternate the petal color combinations in each group of flowers as you continue the design. Let some of the background show through. Let petals overlap the edges of the background.
5. Paint four-dot centers and the stems with Limeade. Let the design dry completely.

Continued on page 117

HYDRANGEA WORKSHEET

Fig. 1:
Slip-slap Emperor Blue +
Royal Purple on background.

Paint other petals with
a filbert brush double
loaded with Lilac Lace
and Tropical Purple.

Double load a
filbert brush with
Emperor Blue +
Royal Purple and
Tropical Purple.
Paint the dark
petals.

Fig. 2:
Paint petals over entire
background. Let some of the
background show through.
Let petals overlap
the edges of
the background.

Paint four-dot centers
with Limeade.

continued from page 104

Wood Hearts (Leaves):

1. Basecoat with Clover. Let dry.
2. Brush on a thick coat of crackle medium, using a foam brush. Let dry.
3. Thin Basil Green with water. Brush over crackle medium. Cracks will form.

Numbers:

1. Basecoat with Maple Syrup. Let dry.
2. Brush on a thick coat of crackle medium, using a foam brush. Let dry.
3. Thin Warm White with water. Brush over numbers. Cracks will form. Let dry completely.
4. Using a dry brush, brush Periwinkle, Orchid, and basil in just a few areas to give the numbers an aged look.

FINISH

1. Apply two coats of clear gloss enamel sealer to the flowers. Let dry between coats.
2. Brush wooden heart and numbers with exterior varnish. Let dry.
3. Glue hearts and numbers to window with waterproof glue.
4. Attach the screw eyes into the top of the window frame.
5. Attach the chain to the screw eyes. ❑

Pattern for Window
Enlarge @ 200% for actual size.

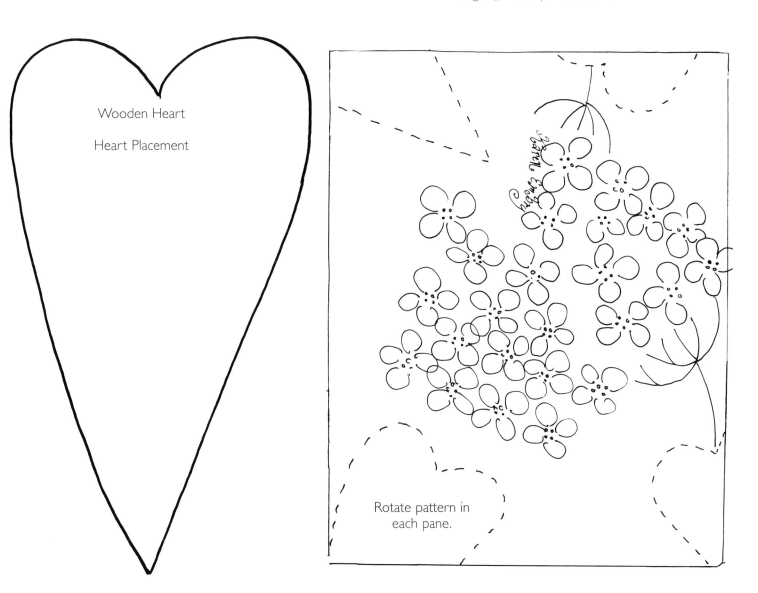

Wooden Heart

Heart Placement

Rotate pattern in each pane.

FOUR SEASONS
storage cabinet

This little cabinet is a great way to teach a child about the seasons. You can use these seasonal motifs in a variety of ways.

COLOR PALETTE

Acrylic Craft Paints (all four seasons):

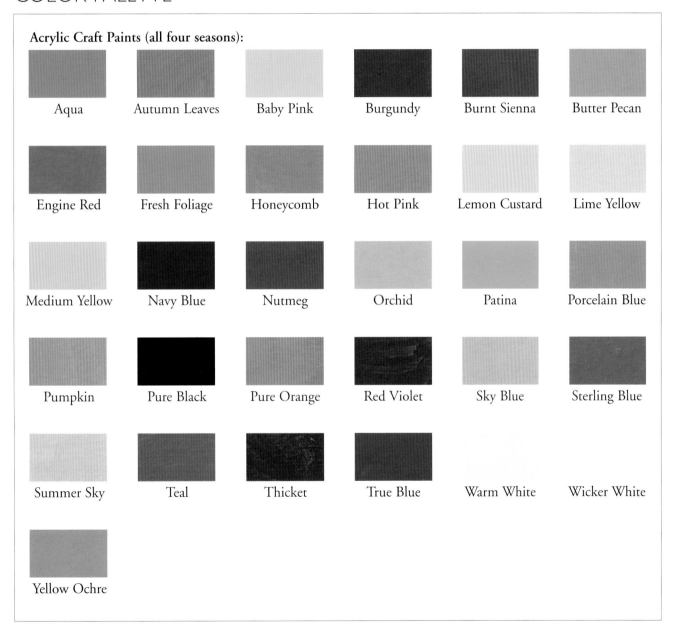

Aqua	Autumn Leaves	Baby Pink	Burgundy	Burnt Sienna	Butter Pecan
Engine Red	Fresh Foliage	Honeycomb	Hot Pink	Lemon Custard	Lime Yellow
Medium Yellow	Navy Blue	Nutmeg	Orchid	Patina	Porcelain Blue
Pumpkin	Pure Black	Pure Orange	Red Violet	Sky Blue	Sterling Blue
Summer Sky	Teal	Thicket	True Blue	Warm White	Wicker White
Yellow Ochre					

Instructions follow on page 120

SURFACE
Wooden four drawer cabinet

BRUSHES
Angulars - 1/8", 1/4", 1/2"

Rounds - sizes 2, 4, 6, 8

Liners - sizes 2, 4

Script Liners - sizes 2/0, 2

Brights - size 6

OTHER SUPPLIES
Permanent fine tip marker - black

Matte sealer spray

PREPARE SURFACE
1. Sand cabinet. Wipe away dust.
2. Seal. Let dry.
3. Base paint cabinet and drawers with Wicker White. Let dry.
4. Transfer the design.

PAINT THE SPRING DRAWER FRONT
Sun:
1. Basecoat with Lemon Custard.
2. Float edges with Yellow Ochre.
3. Dry brush Warm White in center.

Bunny:
1. Basecoat with Warm White.
2. Float edges and curves with Butter Pecan.
3. Paint nose and outline tail with Butter Pecan.
4. Paint eye with Pure Black. Add a tiny Warm White highlight.
5. Paint inside ears with Baby Pink.

Flower:
See the Spring Worksheet.
1. Basecoat petals with Orchid.
2. Float outer edge of each petal with Warm White.
3. Float inside edge of each petal near center with Red Violet.
4. Dry brush Warm White in centers of petals.
5. Paint lines in petals coming from center with Red Violet.
6. Basecoat center with Lemon Custard.
7. Float edges of center with Yellow Ochre.
8. Dry brush center with Warm White.

9. Paint the lips and dry brush the cheeks with Hot Pink.
10. Paint eyes with Pure Black. Paint tiny highlights in eyes with Wicker White.

Leaves & Grass:
1. Basecoat with Lime Yellow.
2. Float bottom edges of leaves and top of grass with Fresh Foliage.
3. Paint grass blades with Fresh Foliage.
4. Paint the veins in leaves with Thicket.

Linework & Lettering:
1. Paint lines around top of drawer with Orchid and Red Violet.
2. Paint the "s" and "n" with Baby Pink and Hot Pink.
3. Paint the "p" with Teal and Sky Blue.
4. Paint the "r" with Red Violet and Orchid.
5. Paint the "i" with Lemon Custard and Yellow Ochre.
6. Paint the "g" with Lime Yellow and Fresh Foliage.

PAINT THE SUMMER DRAWER FRONT
Palm Tree:
See the Summer Worksheet.
1. Basecoat the palm fronds with Fresh Foliage.
2. Float tops of fronds with Lime Yellow.
3. Paint tips of fronds with Thicket.
4. Highlights fronds with Wicker White.
5. Paint trunk with Honeycomb.
6. Float one edge with Nutmeg.

Water:
1. Basecoat with Patina.
2. Float top edges of waves with Aqua.
3. Highlights with Wicker White.

Flag:
1. Paint stripes on flag with Engine Red and Wicker White.
2. Paint upper left corner of flag with True Blue.
3. Float bottom of blue corner with Navy Blue.
4. Paint stars with Wicker White.
5. Float bottom of red stripes with Burgundy.
6. Paint flagpole with Honeycomb.

Beach Ball:
1. Paint two opposite sections with Engine Red, True Blue, Lemon Custard, and Fresh Foliage.
2. Float the edges of the red sections with Burgundy.
3. Float the edges of the blue sections with Navy Blue.
4. Float the edges of the yellow sections with Yellow Ochre.
5. Float the edges of the green sections with Thicket.

Linework & Lettering:
1. Paint lines around the top with Lemon Custard and Yellow Ochre.
2. Paint the "s" and the second "m" with Engine Red and Burgundy.
3. Paint the "u" and the "r" with True Blue and Summer Sky.
4. Paint the first "m" with Patina and Aqua.
5. Paint the "e" with Fresh Foliage and Thicket.

PAINT THE FALL DRAWER FRONT

Jack o' Lantern:
See the Fall Worksheet.
1. Basecoat with Pumpkin.
2. Float the edges of the sections with Autumn Leaves.
3. Paint the stem with Honeycomb.
4. Float one side of the stem with Nutmeg.
5. Paint the tendril next to the stem and swirl on stem with Nutmeg.
6. Paint leaf with Fresh Foliage.
7. Float the bottom edge of the leaf with Thicket.
8. Paint veins in leaf with Thicket.
9. Highlight leaf and stem with Wicker White. Paint eyes with Wicker White.
10. Paint pupils, nose, and mouth with Pure Black.

Ground:
1. Basecoat with Pumpkin.
2. Float the top edge with Medium Yellow.
3. Float bottom edge with Autumn Leaves.

Leaves:
1. Basecoat the back leaf with Autumn Leaves.
2. Float bottom and center of this leaf with Burnt Sienna.
3. Basecoat front leaf with Pumpkin.
4. Float bottom and center of this leaf with Autumn Leaves.
5. Highlight both leaves with Wicker White.

Linework & lettering:
1. Paint lines at top of drawer with Autumn Leaves and Pumpkin.
2. Paint the "F" and the first "l" with Autumn Leaves and Pumpkin.
3. Paint the "a" with Engine Red and Burgundy.
4. Paint the second "l" with Yellow Ochre and Nutmeg.

PAINT THE WINTER DRAWER FRONT

Tree:
1. Basecoat the tree with Fresh Foliage.
2. Float the bottom of each tree section with Thicket.
3. Basecoat the star with Lemon Custard.
4. Float the bottom of the star with Yellow Ochre.
5. Basecoat the trunk with Honeycomb.
6. Float the bottom of the trunk with Nutmeg.

Snowman:
See the Winter Worksheet.
1. Basecoat the snowman with Wicker White.
2. Float the tops of the hills and around the three sections of the snowman with Porcelain Blue.
3. Paint snowman's scarf with Engine Red.
4. Paint lines and dots on scarf with Wicker White.
5. Paint nose with Pure Orange.
6. Float bottom of nose with Engine Red.
7. Paint the snowman's arms with Nutmeg.
8. Highlight arms with Honeycomb.
9. Paint buttons with Pure Black.
10. Highlight buttons with Wicker White.
11. Dry brush cheeks with Hot Pink.

Linework & lettering:
1. Paint the lines around the top with Porcelain Blue and Sterling Blue.
2. Paint the "W", "n", "e" with Porcelain Blue and Sterling Blue.
3. Paint the "i", "t", and "r" with Engine Red and Burgundy.
4. Paint the snowflakes with Porcelain Blue. Let dry completely.

FINISH

1. Draw the lines for the flower's mouth on the Spring Drawer with the black marker.
2. Draw lines at the side of the jack o'lantern's mouth and the eyebrows on the Fall Drawer with the black marker.
3. Draw the snowman's mouth, eyes, and eyebrows on the Winter Drawer with the black marker.
4. Lightly mist the drawer fronts with matte sealer. Let dry. Apply a second coat. Let dry. ❑

Spring & Summer Worksheet

SPRING

Fig. 1:

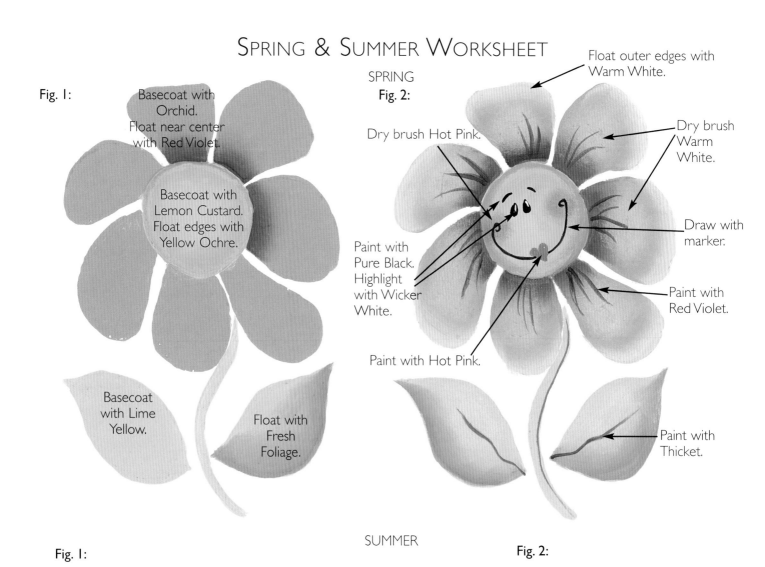

Basecoat with Orchid. Float near center with Red Violet.

Basecoat with Lemon Custard. Float edges with Yellow Ochre.

Basecoat with Lime Yellow.

Float with Fresh Foliage.

Fig. 2:

Float outer edges with Warm White.

Dry brush Hot Pink.

Dry brush Warm White.

Draw with marker.

Paint with Pure Black. Highlight with Wicker White.

Paint with Red Violet.

Paint with Hot Pink.

Paint with Thicket.

SUMMER

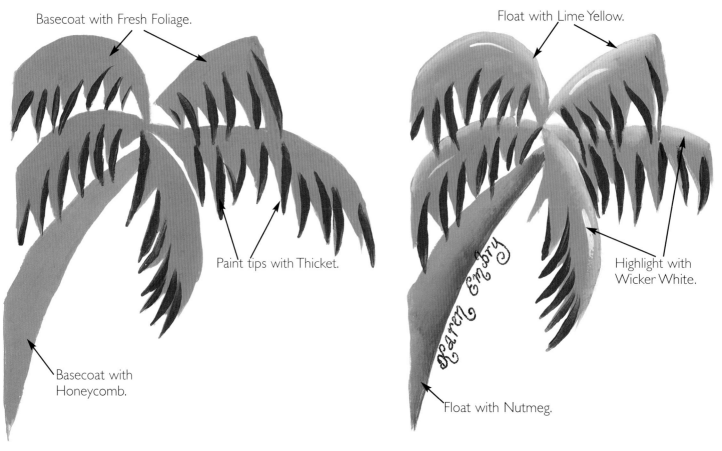

Fig. 1:

Basecoat with Fresh Foliage.

Paint tips with Thicket.

Basecoat with Honeycomb.

Fig. 2:

Float with Lime Yellow.

Highlight with Wicker White.

Karen Embry

Float with Nutmeg.

Fall & Winter Worksheet

FALL

Fig. 1:

Basecoat with Fresh Foliage. Float with Thicket.

Basecoat with Honeycomb. Float stem with Nutmeg.

Basecoat with Pumpkin.

Paint with Wicker White.

Paint with Pure Black.

Fig. 2:

Paint swirl with Nutmeg.

Paint with Thicket.

Highlight with Wicker White.

Draw with black marker.

WINTER

Fig. 1:

Basecoat with Nutmeg.

Basecoat with Wicker White.

Float body with Porcelain Blue.

Basecoat with Engine Red.

Fig. 2:

Highlight with Honeycomb.

Draw with black marker.

Basecoat with Pure Orange. Float bottom with Engine Red.

Add details with Wicker White.

Paint with Pure Black. Highlight with Wicker White.

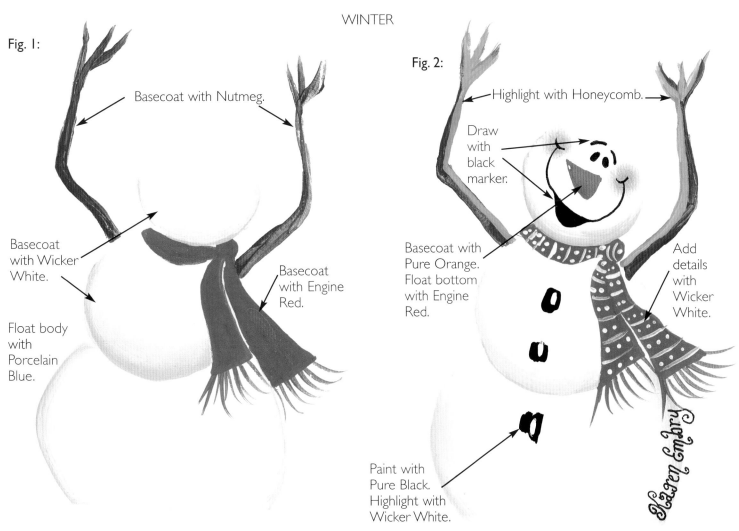

Patterns for Storage Cabinet
(Actual Size)

Karen Embry

Patterns continue on next page

126

Enlarge @ 130% for actual size.

METRIC CONVERSION CHART

Inches to Millimeters and Centimeters

Inches	MM	CM	Inches	MM	CM
1/8	3	.3	2	51	5.1
1/4	6	.6	3	76	7.6
3/8	10	1.0	4	102	10.2
1/2	13	1.3	5	127	12.7
5/8	16	1.6	6	152	15.2
3/4	19	1.9	7	178	17.8
7/8	22	2.2	8	203	20.3
1	25	2.5	9	229	22.9
1-1/4	32	3.2	10	254	25.4
1-1/2	38	3.8	11	279	27.9
1-3/4	44	4.4	12	305	30.5

Yards to Meters

Yards	Meters
1/8	.11
1/4	.23
3/8	.34
1/2	.46
5/8	.57
3/4	.69
7/8	.80
1	.91
2	1.83
3	2.74
4	3.66
5	4.57
6	5.49
7	6.40
8	7.32
9	8.23
10	9.14

INDEX